Profitable Pricing Strategies

Profitable Pricing Strategies

Stephen L. Montgomery

McGraw-Hill Book Company
New York   St. Louis   San Francisco   Auckland   Bogotá
Hamburg   London   Madrid   Mexico   Milan
Montreal   New Delhi   Panama   Paris   São Paulo
Singapore   Sydney   Tokyo   Toronto

Library of Congress Cataloging-in-Publication Data

Montgomery, Steve.
  Profitable pricing strategies.

  Bibliography: p.
  Includes index.
  1. Pricing. I. Title.
HF5416.5.M67 1988   658.8'16   87-4089
ISBN 0-07-042860-3

1234567890 DOC/DOC 89321098

ISBN 0-07-042860-3

*The editors for this book were William A. Sabin and Jim Bessent,
the designer was Naomi Auerbach, and the production
supervisor was Richard A. Ausburn. It was set in Baskerville
by Digitype, Inc.*

Printed and bound by R. R. Donnelley & Sons Company.

To Carolyn

For her inspiration and support

Contents

Preface

Profitable Pricing Strategies is designed to help managers learn and make profitable use of the critical skills of planning and managing pricing activities. An accompanying software package, PricePlan, will help users of this book choose from among several alternative strategies as well as explore the economic implications of any given price strategy.

In this book, I try to give the reader a timely introduction to the management of price strategy, based on well-accepted theories, and a strong focus on actual applications. Concepts are drawn from marketing, economics, finance, and accounting, and are developed in a strategic management framework.

The reader is introduced in Chapter 1 to the strategic management process. Overall organizational strategic management is presented, and then the management of marketing, operations, finance, and other functional strategies are discussed, with emphasis placed on marketing. The components of the entire process are displayed graphically and related to each other.

Chapter 2 relates pricing strategy to the overall strategy of an organization and its functional support groups. Pricing strategy is discussed in some detail, down to the process of actually selecting a price strategy.

Later chapters cover special topics under pricing strategy. New product and service pricing, an important subject for almost any organization, is discussed in Chapter 3.

Chapter 4 explores the pricing process for groups of related products or services, usually referred to as the product line. Economics of the interrelationships among products is presented, and cost considerations in pricing are discussed.

The subject of planning and managing under conditions of uncertainty affects almost all organizations which must price their offerings to the marketplace. The factors involved in determining the actual market demand for products and services are examined, along with some methods for analyzing these factors.

This leads naturally into Chapter 6, which covers price forecasting. Price forecasting is often difficult to do. Chapter 6 provides an overview of the forecasting process in general, from the level of the overall economy down to the level of individual products and services. Many of the most widely used forecasting methods are presented here.

Service organizations are very often ignored in discussions of business planning and management, so Chapter 7 discusses services in relation to physical products or goods. Practical service pricing considerations (which often apply to physical products) are discussed in some detail.

A solid economic foundation is required for effective pricing. Chapter 8 presents cost-volume-profit analysis and some analytical methods often used to set and manage prices.

Today more than ever pricing and strategic management need to be considered in a world view. Chapter 9 discusses international pricing and the complex factors involved in selling products and services worldwide.

Chapter 10 covers the economics of price and costs, in more general terms than does Chapter 8. Special topics of pricing are covered in Chapter 11: pricing and profit maximization, pricing and promotion, pricing and marketing channels (often called distribution channels), price discrimination, and transfer pricing. Chapter 12 wraps up discussions of price strategy by giving the reader ideas on how to implement strategic plans.

I hope that the readers of this book can share my enthusiasm for the power that careful strategic planning and management can give managers in all types of business organizations. I firmly believe that readers of this book can become better pricing managers simply by getting down to basics and working smarter, not harder. It is hoped that this book and other books and software products I am developing to deal with strategic management issues will give readers numerous profitable ideas, and that the readers will be stimulated to do further reading, research, and effective business practice.

Stephen L. Montgomery

Acknowledgements

This book was inspired by my work with business and nonprofit organizations, my teaching experiences, and my work at Planning Professionals, Inc., of Milwaukee, Wisconsin.

I owe a lot to a good friend of mine, Frank Koch, who helped me to develop the PricePlan software package. Frank and his wife Pat helped me with many administrative tasks during the book's development, and helped me coordinate numerous consulting and teaching tasks.

My parents have been a great help to me for innumerable reasons. My wife Carolyn missed much of the early work on this book but has been a tremendous inspiration and an avid supporter since I first met her.

Stephen L. Montgomery

1
Pricing and Organizational Planning

Pricing cannot be viewed in isolation, but rather must be viewed in the context of a much larger framework. It is only one aspect of marketing, albeit a very important one, and is part of the overall planning for any organization.

Pricing is an important expression of your marketing plan and is a communication to the marketplace of your philosophy. Your philosophy is transformed into your organization's strategic plan. The strategic plan then generates or changes the marketing plan. A circular planning process is created, a primary thrust of which is your organization's pricing policy.

Pricing may reflect whether your organization is targeting the retail or the business market and whether you want to be a full-product or full-service supplier to all customers or a supplier to specific target-market segments. If you want to be the dominant market-share leader in all the markets you serve, then your prices will reflect this.

Marketing is the process of integrating buyer needs and wants into your organization's market strategy and producing products and services to fulfill these needs and wants while earning a profit (if yours is a profit-oriented organization) or satisfying other organizational objectives (if yours is a nonprofit organization).

The Strategic Management Process

Strategic management consists of a set of decisions and actions which result in the formulation and implementation of strategies designed to achieve the objectives of an organization (see Fig. 1.1). The following areas must be addressed:

1. Determine the mission of your organization, including broad statements about your purpose, philosophy, and goals.

2. Develop your organization profile, reflecting its capabilities and limitations.

3. Assess your organization's external environment.

4. Analyze possible opportunities.

5. Identify desired options consistent with the organizational mission.

6. Choose a particular set of long-term objectives and grand strategies to achieve desired options.

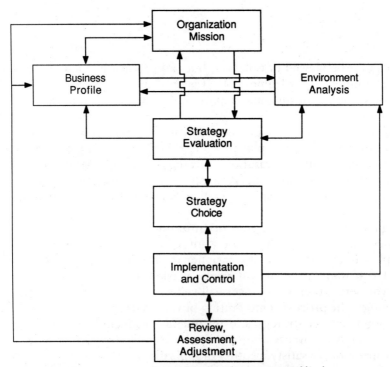

Figure 1.1. The strategic management process at the organizational level.

7. Develop annual objectives and short-term strategies compatible with long-term objectives and grand strategies.

8. Implement strategic-choice decisions based on resources.

9. Review and evaluate the success of the strategic process and input results into future decision making.

Bower (1966) suggests that the following specific management activities exist in the strategic management process:

1. Setting the organizational mission
2. Developing an organizational philosophy
3. Establishing objectives
4. Planning strategy
5. Establishing policies
6. Planning the organizational structure
7. Providing personnel
8. Establishing procedures
9. Providing facilities
10. Providing capital
11. Setting standards
12. Establishing management programs and operational plans
13. Providing control information
14. Activating people

Organizational Mission

Your first prerequisite for marketing planning is a statement of your organizational mission. This should define the kind of organization you wish to have and should identify customers and markets you want to serve. Your mission statement should tell everyone in your organization what *business* you are in. It focuses attention on the direction for the future. Your mission defines the bounds within which you look for viable marketing opportunities, and it may be assigned to divisions.

According to King and Cleland (1979), an organization mission is designed to

1. Ensure unanimity of purpose within the organization
2. Provide a basis for motivating organizational resources

3. Develop a standard for allocating resources

4. Establish a general organizational climate

5. Serve as a focal point for those who can identify with the organization's purpose and direction, and as an explication to deter those who cannot from participating further in the organization's actions

6. Facilitate translation of objectives and goals into a work breakdown structure involving assignment of tasks to responsible elements in the organization

7. Provide a specification of organizational purposes and translation of them into goals so that cost, time, and performance parameters can be assessed and controlled

Organizational Profile

Your organizational profile results from an internal analysis which determines your performance capabilities based on existing or obtainable resources. This profile describes the quality and quantity of physical, financial, and human resources available to you and assesses your organization's management and structural strengths and weaknesses. Historical successes and management views are contrasted with your current capabilities in order to identify future capabilities.

Remote and Local Environments

Your external environment consists of the total of all forces which affect your strategic options but which are beyond your ability to control. The remote environment is composed of forces which occur beyond your immediate operating environment and includes the general economic, political, social, and technological framework in which you and your competitors operate (see Fig. 1.2)

The local environment includes forces in your specific competitive operating situation which influence your strategy selections. Changes in the local environment are often the result of actions taken by you, your competitors, consumers or users, suppliers, creditors, or government bodies (see Fig. 1.3).

Analyzing Opportunities

Assessing your expected environment and your organizational profile enables you to determine the range of opportunities that you might want to take advantage of. These opportunities represent possible directions, but the list of alternatives must be screened before a set of possible choices can be decided upon. This strategic choice process provides you with a combination of long-term objectives and grand strategy that will best position your organization in the external environment and achieve your organizational mission.

The process of choosing from among alternative strategies involves matching each of the possible and desirable opportunities with reasonable long-term objectives and targets. These are then matched with the most

---

Economic

    Regional, national, and international markets—availability, change

    Interest rates, capital availability, credit availability, income, savings, expenses

    Shifts in the above economic factors

    Shifts in demand for product categories

Social

    Attitudes and values regarding marriage, lifestyle, work, ethics, sex roles, childbearing, racial equality, education, retirement, pollution, energy

    Effect of population changes on social and political expectations at home and abroad

    Constraints and opportunities development

Political

    Changes in U.S. government policy regarding antitrust, foreign trade, taxation, depreciation, environmental protection, deregulation, defense, foreign trade barriers, etc.

    Effectiveness of government administration.

    International political environment: hostile or favorable, stable, corrupt, violent, strongly nationalistic, etc.

    International governmental policies regarding trade barriers, equity requirements, patent protection, etc.

Technology

    Current state-of-the-art

    Feasible new products or services

    Impact of technological breakthroughs in related product areas

    Interfaces with economic and social values, public safety, governmental regulations, and court interpretations

Adapted from *Strategic Management: Strategy Formulation and Implementation* by Pearce and Robinson, Richard D. Irwin, Inc., Homewood, IL, 1982, pp. 133–134.

Figure 1.2. External environment considerations.

promising targets (grand strategies) for achieving the desired results. Each alternative is then evaluated to determine the one you expect to best achieve your organizational mission.

Assessing strategic alternatives requires that you develop criteria to serve as the basis for comparing one alternative with all of the others. The criteria you use might include your attitudes about risk, stability, flexibility, profitability, growth, and diversification. Also, you should consider

1. The volatility of the external environment

2. Your current organizational structure

3. Your access to resources

4. Your competitive advantages

5. Product or service life-cycle stages

Competitive Position

Probability of new competitors, new product substitutes

Strategic moves of existing rivals

Competitive priorities and ability to change competitors' minds (steer their actions)

Predictability of competitors' actions

Customer Profiles

Customer needed value

Formal versus informal market research results

How are customer needs now being met?

Marketing channels available

Market segmentation opportunities

Suppliers and Creditors

Likelihood of major cost increases due to reduced sources of supply, funding, personnel, or other production constraints

Reliability of existing supplies

Likely responses of suppliers and creditors to special emergency requests

Labor

Availability of employees with needed skills and abilities in geographic areas

Existence of nearby colleges and vocational schools to aid training

Cooperation of labor unions

Adapted from *Strategic Management: Strategy Formulation and Implementation* by Pearce and Robinson, Richard D. Irwin, Inc., Homewood, IL, 1982, pp. 136–137.

Figure 1.3. Local environment considerations.

6. The potential reaction of stockholders, creditors, employees, customers, suppliers, governments, unions, competitors, local communities, or the general public

Objectives and Strategies

After the mission statement, you must clearly define your overall objectives in order to design organizational and marketing strategies to obtain these objectives. You might set an organizational goal to attain a certain financial goal. Or you might adopt a more general objective, such as to play a certain role in your industry. You might want to gain a certain market share or achieve a certain level of innovation or technological advancement.

Top management must set the overall objectives for the organization, and the lower levels of management must set goals to support the organizational objectives. The hierarchy of objectives and goals extends down through the organization until detailed action programs can be designed and implemented at every level.

Long-term Objectives. Your long-term objectives are the results you seek to achieve over a period of, say, five years. These results are typically developed to address these and other issues:

1. Profitability
2. Competitive position
3. Productivity
4. Technological superiority
5. Employee development

For maximum effectiveness, each objective must be specific, measurable, achievable, and consistent with your other objectives.

Grand Strategy. Your grand strategy is your comprehensive, general plan of action by which you intend to achieve your long-term objectives. This statement indicates how your goals of business activity are to be achieved. The purpose of grand strategies is to guide the acquisition and allocation of resources over a specified period of time.

No single grand strategy can detail the strategic actions which you will undertake over a long period, but your commitment to a basic positioning of your organization in your marketplace provides you with a focal point for later decision making. Some examples of grand strategies include technological innovation to capture high profit margin on new products, retrenchment to avoid bankruptcy, and diversification to enable growth through acquisition of related businesses (see Fig. 1.4).

Short-term Objectives.   Results which you expect to achieve within, say, one year are your short-term objectives. These goals are more specific than long-term objectives because they help you to determine your short-term strategies for day-to-day operations. Companywide short-term objectives should be reflected in the planning of all major functions and divisions of your organization. Research and development, finance, marketing, and production departments must be able to work to achieve short-term organizational objectives.

Operating Strategies.   Under the general framework of grand strategy, specific plans of action are needed for each business function or division. You normally will try to develop an operating strategy for each of your short-term objectives. There will be an operating strategy for marketing to indicate how the annual objectives will be achieved, one for production, and one for each of the functional areas of your organization. These operating strategies will be used to achieve objectives within the immediate future, perhaps one year. Your organization's budgeting will be coordinated with department operating strategies. Refer to Fig. 1.5 for a list of internal strategic factors to consider when planning operating strategies. Figures 1.6, 1.7, 1.8, and 1.9 illustrate the interrelationships of operating strategies by business function.

Strategy Implementation

This strategy planning stage involves acquiring and allocating resources and developing structures and procedures necessary to make a strategy operational. Implementation involves assignment of responsibility to appropriate employees, with allocation of required resources, thereby putting the strategies into action. Five variables should be considered here:

1. Responsibilities
2. People
3. Structures
4. Technology
5. Rewards

To successfully implement organizational strategies, you must effectively design and manage methods which will integrate all pertinent factors into your organization's actions. One of your major priorities in

Concentration

1. Increase product or service usage.
   a. Increase purchase size.
   b. Speed up product or service obsolescence.
   c. Promote other uses.
   d. Reduce price for increased use.

2. Win customers from competition.
   a. Sharpen product or service differentiation.
   b. Increase promotion.
   c. Cut prices.

3. Attract nonusers.
   a. Use sampling and price inducements.
   b. Change prices.
   c. Promote new uses.

Market Development

1. Open markets in new locations.
   a. Expand regionally.
   b. Expand nationally.
   c. Expand internationally.

2. Target new market segments.
   a. Develop new product or service versions.
   b. Use new marketing channels.
   c. Promote in previously unused media.

Product Development

1. Develop new product or service features
   a. Adapt
   b. Modify
   c. Magnify
   d. Reduce
   e. Substitute
   f. Rearrange
   g. Reverse
   h. Combine

2. Develop quality variations.

3. Develop new models and sizes.

Adapted from *Strategic Management: Strategy Formulation and Implementation* by Pearce and Robinson, Richard E. Irwin, Inc., Homewood, IL, 1982, p. 191.

Figure 1.4. Grand strategic options.

Figure 1.5. Internal strategic factors.

Marketing

   1. Breadth of product line
   2. Ability to gather market information
   3. Market shares established or desired
   4. Product or service mix
   5. Marketing channels in use or available
   6. Sales organization effectiveness
   7. Sales concentrations by product or customer
   8. Product or service image, reputation, and quality
   9. Marketing communications — message style, media chosen
  10. Pricing strategy chosen
  11. Ability to develop new products or services or markets
  12. Postscale service and follow-up available
  13. Goodwill and brand loyalty established or desired

Finance and Accounting

   1. Ability to raise short-term and long-term capital
   2. Organization-level resources
   3. Cost of capital relative to costs incurred by competitors
   4. Taxes
   5. Owners and investors — return on equity
   6. Financial leverage — debt/equity ratio
   7. Barriers to and costs of market entry
   8. Planning and budgeting activities needed
   9. Working capital available
  10. Cost controls in effect

Operations

   1. Raw materials, component parts, and supplies
   2. Inventory control
   3. Facilities
   4. Subcontracting
   5. Vertical integration
   6. Equipment
   7. Technology
   8. Operations control
   9. Legal protections

Personnel

   1. Management
   2. Employees
   3. Labor relations

---

4. Policies
5. Incentives
6. Hiring schedules
7. Turnover and absenteeism
8. Specialized skills
9. Experience levels

General Organization

1. Organization structure
2. Image and prestige
3. Achieving objectives
4. Communication
5. Control systems
6. Organization climate
7. Systematic decision making
8. Top management

Adapted from *Strategic Management: Strategy Formulation and Implementation* by Pearce and Robinson, Richard D. Irwin, Inc., Homewood, IL, 1982, pp. 163–164.

implementation involves the synchronization of the acquisition and allocation of resources with the actions taken during the planning process.

Review and Evaluation

A strategy which has been implemented must be monitored in order to determine the extent of progress made toward the objectives. Formulating a strategy requires that you watch for early signs of the responsiveness of your environment to the strategies. You must find ways to monitor and control implementation to ensure that your strategic plan is being followed correctly. Remember: Your organization is only successful when your strategies achieve your objectives. Among the measures of strategy success are the following:

Return on equity	Market share
Return on assets	Sales growth
Net profit	Customer satisfaction
Asset growth	Return on sales
Production costs	Sales per employee
Production growth	Profit per employee
Stock price	Employee satisfaction
Earnings per share	Value added

Liquidity Ratios

1. Current ratio $= \dfrac{\text{current assets}}{\text{current liabilities}}$

2. Net working capital $=$ current assets $-$ current liabilities

3. Quick ratio $= \dfrac{\text{current assets} - \text{inventory}}{\text{current liabilities}}$

4. Cash/average-daily-purchases ratio $= \dfrac{\text{cash}}{\text{annual purchases}/360}$

Activity Ratios

5. Inventory turnover $= \dfrac{\text{cost of goods or services sold}}{\text{beginning inventory} - \text{ending inventory}}$

6. Averge collection period $= \dfrac{\text{receivables}}{\text{credit sales}/360}$

7. Asset turnover $= \dfrac{\text{sales}}{\text{operating assets}}$

Leverage Ratios

8. Percentage of debt financing $= \dfrac{\text{total debt}}{\text{total assets}}$

9. Debt/equity ratio $= \dfrac{\text{total debt}}{\text{total assets}}$

10. Times fixed charges earned $= \dfrac{\text{earnings before interest \& tax}}{\text{fixed charges}}$

11. Cash flow coverage $= \dfrac{\text{earnings before interest tax} + \text{deprec.}}{\text{interest} + [\text{payment}/(1 - \text{tax rate})]}$

Profitability Ratios

12. Return on investment $= \dfrac{\text{net operating income}}{\text{operating assets}}$

13. Operating margin $= \dfrac{\text{net operating income}}{\text{sales}}$

14. Return on common stock $= \dfrac{\text{net profit}}{\text{net worth}}$

15. Earnings per share $= \dfrac{\text{net income} - \text{preferred stock dividends}}{\text{number of common shares outstanding}}$

16. Price/earnings ratio $= \dfrac{\text{market price of common stock}}{\text{earnings per share}}$

17. Dividend yield $= \dfrac{\text{common dividends per share}}{\text{market price of common stock}}$

18. Dividend payout $= \dfrac{\text{common dividends per share}}{\text{common stock earnings per share}}$

Figure 1.6. Summary of financial ratios useful in strategic planning and control.

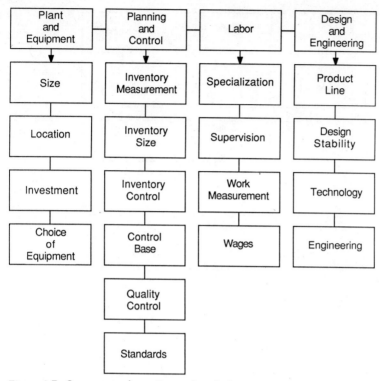

Figure 1.7. Components of operations and production strategy.

Long-Run Marketing Strategy

If your organization is a large one, the next stage of strategic planning management takes place at the level of a division or business group which is responsible for a portion of your organization's overall business. A division might be an internal entity, such as a department, or an external entity, such as a separate subsidiary company.

Marketing planning responsibility at the division level is to develop an overall marketing strategy or long-range plan. There is no single method to follow in developing and implementing the marketing strategy, but the following discussion should give you some ideas about how to approach this process.

Analyze Your Marketing Situation

After you have analyzed your organization and its environment, you should conduct a situation analysis of your marketing situation. First, you

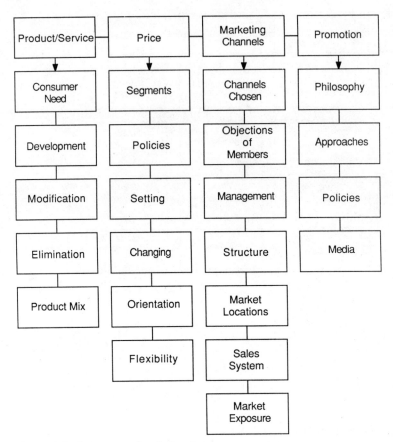

Figure 1.8. Components of marketing strategy.

must periodically review your organization's strengths and weaknesses in light of your marketing capabilities and constraints. You must evaluate your past performance as well as your marketing strengths and weaknesses. In particular, pay close attention to your product line, your distribution channels, your promotional effectiveness, and, of course, your pricing.

You will then need to use market-research techniques to answer questions that arise regarding management decisions you need to make. Third, you will conduct sales and cost studies. Next, you will forecast your industry and company sales.

Your sales forecast results from analysis of your economic environment and uses various types of forecasting methods. As you will see in the chapter on forecasting, an early stage of the planning process is a forecast of general business conditions. From this estimate, you can predict both industry sales and those of your organization. From the sales forecast, you can build a profit forecast based on revenues and costs associated with the predicted level of sales.

The sales and profit forecasts at this point are estimates of what you will experience if you continue with your present strategy. You can compare this forecast with your objectives to discover if a planning gap exists. If a gap does exist, you should consider modifying your present strategy. For additional information, refer to the coverage of demand measurement and forecasting in Chapter 6.

Assess Your Opportunities and Constraints

This step in marketing planning involves interpreting the results of your situation analysis, including facts about the economy, your industry, indi-

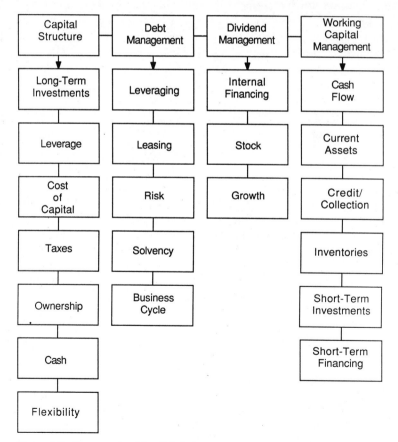

Figure 1.9. Components of financial strategy.

vidual consumers or users, and other external-environment factors. You
must identify specific marketing management opportunities that can be
used as practical guides to your operational planning. You might find
opportunities to create a new kind of competitive advantage, to innovate
technically, or to gain a new market niche.

Identify Target Market Segments

Assessing opportunities and problems will likely enable you to identify
several target market segments. This selection process is influenced by the
importance of the market segment to your organization's objectives, the
potential for success which the segment represents, and your organization's capacity to reach the segment. Consumers or users comprising a
particular target market segment are unique. Older consumers are different with respect to their fashions than are teenagers, for instance.

Each market segment will respond differently to your marketing efforts,
so you will not always approach segments in the same manner. Simply
recognizing that certain markets can be segmented is important to your
planning, because each major segment will likely require its own marketing strategy.

Determine the Level of
Commitment Required

You must be concerned with the allocation of limited resources among
your alternative target markets and product or service items. Usually, you
will determine the level of resource commitment required by identifying
activities required to reach your targets. Obviously, reaching some segments will be more costly than reaching others, and you have only a limited
amount of resources to expend. You have limited financial resources,
production capacity, personnel resources, and sources of supply.

The priority of the target market segments affects your decisions. A
low-priority segment which would require the majority of your marketing
resources would probably be rejected, but you might choose a high-prior-
ity segment even though it would significantly drain your resources. You
may need to choose some programs in order to respond quickly to competitors. Plans which are not urgent and can be safely postponed can be
temporarily rejected.

The level of risk among alternative programs may heavily influence
your decisions. Investing in marketing programs is akin to investing in
production plant and equipment and other capital investments. Segments
offering similar opportunity and cost might exhibit different risk levels, in
which case you might choose the lower-risk projects. You must combine

your subjective feelings with known facts about the alternatives from which you must choose.

Choosing a Grand Strategy

As with the organizational grand strategy, you must develop a grand strategy for your overall marketing plan. You need to conceive one or more complete alternative marketing plans to guide your operations.

You might want to develop a promotional line of products or services, designed to compete entirely on a price basis with your established product or service line and with competitive low-priced items. Segmentation on the basis of quality might prevent sales of your existing lines from suffering.

Another alternative might involve the design of a new product line differentiated by quality. This prestige line would contrast dramatically with your standard line. Emphasis could be on luxury, with promotional and pricing strategies consistent with the product or service and its packaging.

Your marketing planner will not develop the alternative plans; these tactical details will be ironed out by lower-level managers. The planner provides a general statement of the approach to follow. Advantages, disadvantages, possibilities, and dangers must be visible, so a general plan of attack should allow lower-level managers to map out a specific path to the goal.

The Marketing Mix

An integrated marketing plan is a complex and comprehensive expression of a total program of action to reach a specific target and to reach your organization's objectives. It involves important decisions about *product, distribution, promotion,* and *price,* which are referred to as *marketing-mix decisions.*

The elements of the marketing mix must be determined, integrated, and coordinated. Then the marketing program is ready for management approval. These individual marketing-mix items will be discussed in greater detail later in this book as they relate to pricing. The integrated marketing plan provides the comprehensive framework for implementing any successful pricing and marketing strategy.

Short-run Marketing Strategy: Tactics

After the elements of the marketing mix have been developed, you must translate the long-run strategic marketing plans into short-run action plans, or tactics. Tactics should include

1. A statement of actions to take
2. Specific personnel responsible for each action
3. A schedule of action implementation
4. A complete budget for each action
5. A list of expected outcomes for each action

Implementation

Tactics must be communicated to people who will execute them. Your plans must be presented to your sales representatives, distributors, retailers, and anyone else responsible for carrying out your short-term plans. If you are successful in motivating these people, you stand a good chance of seeing your plans do well. If not, you may need to revise your plans to ensure adequate success.

Monitor the Results and Revise as Necessary

The last step in the planning process involves monitoring your plans as they are put into action. Information must be fed back into the planning process in order to determine if your programs are working adequately. If you detect the need for adjustment of tactics or revision of long-run strategies, you must make the changes as soon as possible in order to stay on target.

This marketing control involves monitoring your organization's sales and those of your industry, buying or use intentions of customers and users, and many other factors, including your price levels, costs, and resulting profits. Since your environment will change, even your best marketing plans will become obsolete eventually, and you will need to be able to make required alterations in your plans quickly. By modifying your tactics quickly and decisively, you can compensate for changes in your environment.

Good marketing control should allow you to detect flaws in your performance soon enough to make critical changes. You may need to have contingency plans ready to implement if your strategies are failing. This is why you must develop alternative strategies during your planning process.

2

Price Planning— Gaining the Decisive Price Position

Pricing decisions, like most decisions, aim to achieve organizational objectives, implement strategies, and conform to policies. Properly understood, pricing has a good deal in common with military science. Like a military commander, you, as a marketer of goods or services, need a sound strategy and a repertoire of tactics. The distinction between strategy and tactics may be subtle, but it is important.

Strategic pricing defines your organization's value image in the eyes of the public. Tactical pricing involves your day-to-day management of the pricing process. For pricing strategy, advance planning is your key to achieving and retaining the initiative rather than being forced to react to competitive pressures. For tactical pricing, thorough knowledge of the marketplace and of the many ways to achieve an objective are your keys. To be successful at marketing, you must combine the tactical marketing skills of a guerrilla fighter with a mastery of the principles of conventional strategic marketing warfare.

Objectives

Your objectives are your desired outcomes and preferred states of affairs. These are the goals, aims, or targets you wish to attain to the extent feasible. Some objectives are ultimate and desired for their own sake. Others are instrumental, sought only because they contribute to other, higher-level goals you have set. Objectives should provide you with direction for action. They should inform your managers of the ends they should pursue. Objectives essentially are lists of tasks to perform. Your managers must know them to know what is expected; if they do not, your organization will lack strategic direction. If members of your organization do not know your organization's objectives, they are not likely to attain these objectives. Some common pricing objectives might be

- To increase profitability by 18 percent in the next period
- To make products or services appear more valuable than they really are
- To undermine efforts of new competitors to gain a marketing foothold
- To discourage competitors from entering your markets
- To get competitors to accept you as price leader
- To restore order in a disorderly market
- To increase market share by 22 percent in the next three years
- To induce customers to purchase at more convenient times

Price Strategy

Price strategy consists of a specific objective, a specific approach to achieving the objective, and action plans to implement the approach. Strategy formulation allows you to achieve your objectives more fully or at lower cost. By capitalizing upon a unique feature of your organization and the marketing situation, you can achieve much more benefit from a given level of resources. Some price strategies to consider might be the following:

- To gain market share by concentrating on selected segments of the market where distributors might be more skillful or more willing to invest resources to increase market penetration
- To gain customer trust by reducing price when your costs decline substantially and this drop can be easily noticed
- To weaken competitors by choosing key market segments in which to launch price promotions
- To win customers from competitors by meeting any genuine offer from the competitors
- To win customers from competitors by offering multiple items at low total price, perhaps including products or services not offered by rivals

You might establish a price band for your products or services that enables you to meet market prices and/or achieve target price objectives. Be sure, however, to take full account of five critical factors that define the range of your strategic pricing options:

- Real costs and profits
- Product or service value to the customer relative to value offered by the competition
- Market segment differences
- Likely competitive reactions
- Your marketing objectives

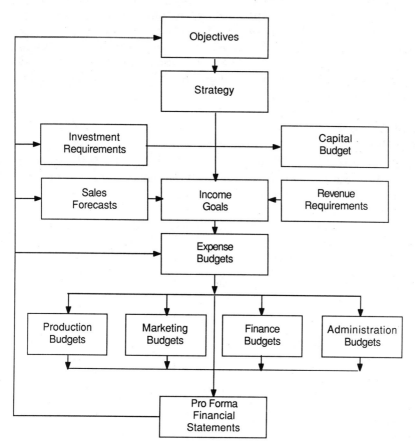

Figure 2.1. Budgeting and the strategic management process.

Real Costs and Profits

If you use fully absorbed production costs to determine your product-line profitability and basic price levels, this approach may leave much to be desired. Fully absorbed production costs are estimated by allocating fixed costs to products along with variable costs, with no regard to direct costs or indirect costs. You might consider turning to an alternative product productivity measure. Contribution pricing acknowledges direct and indirect costs explicitly. The contribution margin (sales minus all variable production, sales, and administrative expenses) gives a more realistic profit figure, making it easy for you to see which products need price increases (and which ones can tolerate price cuts) to achieve market share or volume objectives.

Using the contribution-margin approach could pay off substantially, especially if you need to work in a narrow profit margin situation. Carefully monitor revenue, cost, and profit at various volume levels using variable costs (out-of-pocket, or marginal costs) and fixed costs for a particular time period. You then get a good idea of what your real economic costs and profits are, as opposed to your accounting, or "paper," costs and profits. Figure 2.1 illustrates how cost and revenue estimates fit into the overall planning process.

Product or Service Value to Your Customers

You should not feel that you must compete on price alone rather than on total value. In setting prices, you should evaluate all the elements of your total product or service package by comparing them with those of your competition. How much a customer will pay is not determined by product characteristics and performance alone. In assessing your product or service value, be sure to consider

- Maintenance costs to the consumer
- Energy consumption of the product or service
- Your customer-service ability
- Your delivery response time
- Product or company prestige
- Product or service innovation
- Personal relationships between you and your customers

One competitive analysis that can be enormously valuable to you is a price and performance matrix analysis. Working with data from user records, user surveys, trade association data, or company tests, you can develop a compound performance-characteristic index which includes

- Performance features
- Maintainability of produce or service
- Average service time required
- Reliability of product or service
- Useful life of product or service
- Other product or service attributes

You can chart or plot prices versus performance for your product or service and those of your competitors to discover why principle competitors have larger market shares than lesser rivals.

Three methods can be used to estimate market perceptions of your product or service offering versus perceptions of your rivals' products:

1. *Direct price rating.*   Ask buyers to rate several products or services by estimating a price for each which they think reflects the total value of buying the item from each supplier.

2. *Direct perceived-value rating.*   Ask buyers to rate several suppliers by allocating 100 points among them and distributing the points to reflect the total value of buying products or services from each supplier.

3. *Diagnosis.*   Ask buyers to rate several product or service offerings on a set of attributes. Have buyers allocate 100 points among several suppliers with respect to each attribute. Then have buyers distribute 100 points to reflect the relative importance of the attributes.

For an example of the diagnostic method, consider Table 2.1. By multiplying importance weights against each supplier's ratings, we find offering A to be perceived as above average, offering B to be about average, and offering C to be below average in perceived value (perceived performance for the money). The supplier of offering A can presumably set a high price for the item because it offers more, according to buyer perceptions. If the supplier wants to price proportional to perceived value, it can charge a higher than average price, according to the degree of perceived value superiority.

Table 2.1. The Diagnostic Method

Attribute	Importance weight	Product or service offerings		
		A	B	C
Durability	17	20	80	20
Reliability	27	33	33	33
Delivery	54	50	25	25
Service	12	55	37	8
(Perceived value)	(100)	(46.41)	(32.25)	(21.34)

SOURCE : Adapted from Kotler, *Principles of Marketing*, 3d ed, 1986.

If you price at less than the perceived value of a product or service, you should be able to gain a higher than average market share, because buyers will feel that they are getting more value for their money by dealing with you. The same effect occurs when you can manage to increase the perceived value of your product or service without having to raise prices proportionately.

Armed with insights from a price and performance analysis, you can begin to decide whether you should invest heavily to differentiate your product from ones available from your competition. If the answer is yes, you could add important performance features to your main product or service to upgrade the value relative to that of competitive items.

You might want to introduce a super-premium, high-priced version to capture the top-of-the-line image and profit margins. Or you might introduce a stripped-down version priced below your rivals' products to preempt competitive entry into the lowest-cost market segment. A strategy of adding value through price and performance innovations can give you a significant competitive advantage.

If you find that it probably wouldn't pay to invest heavily to differentiate your product or service items from competitive offerings, you could examine new uses for your products or services, or new types of users. Market segmentation analysis, closely coordinated with pricing strategy, can help you to examine these alternatives. (A software product for this type of analysis is also available from KM Software Solutions.)

Another useful technique for pricing strategy analysis is ranking competitive products by key customer buying factors. After conducting interviews or surveys with existing and prospective customers (or by educated management guessing), you can, for a given product or service, assign weights to each of several product or service buying factors and then rank the performance of each of the competitive offerings against your own.

You should learn that you have certain significant value advantages (and disadvantages) versus your competition, often (but not always) deriving from

- Superior product or service features
- Greater product or service availability
- Better company sales support
- Good personal relationships between your company and its customers
- Product or service modifiability
- Greater ease of product or service use

Your prices might be very close to those of a rival offering. You might be able to estimate whether offering a certain value advantage increase (or decrease) will suffice to gain (or avoid loss of) market share. If so, you can change prices accordingly.

Market-Segment Differences

Price differentiation among customer or market segment groups can be an important key to profit. You might charge end users more for a product or service than you charge customers who add markup costs to your offering. If a replacement part or repeat business will be needed, you might charge customers less to ensure that they obtain the needed parts or business from your company. If your product or service is custom-made or modified for a customer and you thus incur different costs, you will probably want to determine prices for each customer individually, so that you can recover your varying costs. Price-differentiation schemes must be planned very carefully, however, because the potential problems could outweigh the possible benefits. The following two points must be considered:

1. Under the Robinson-Patman Act, the antitrust laws, and certain state "loss-leader" laws, a number of pricing practices present legal pitfalls, including

   - Resale price maintenance — "fair trade" pricing
   - Below-cost reductions — "dumping"
   - Price leadership — keeping prices low can be illegal if it is seen as damaging competition in the long run
   - Price signaling — "loss leader" pricing (legal except if considered predatory toward small competitors)
   - Price discrimination — not always legal unless justified by different costs to sell to different buyers
   - New market entry pricing

2. Those companies that attempt to maintain different price levels for different customers or customer groups often find that strong controls are needed to prevent pressures from the sales force from pulling prices down to the lowest customer level.

Price differentiation schemes, when used, generally result in higher profits by enabling a company to optimize price and volume trade-offs. It is imperative that you understand your real costs, make careful competitive comparisons, and segment your customer groups properly in order to achieve consistent marketing success.

Likely Competitive Reactions

You are courting disaster if you make pricing decisions without carefully taking into account potential competitive retaliatory actions. Reducing prices in your fringe markets or market segments might win you customers in these areas, but if your competitors in these same areas respond by going after customers in your core markets or segments, a devastating price war could result. You should probably make some of your price moves quietly and selectively, so you do not arouse the competition.

You should consider changing your prices only after reviewing competitors' reactions to past price moves. In assessing how a rival might react to a price move, you need to weigh several factors:

- Competitive cost structures
- Past competitive price behavior
- Market demand (or lack of it)
- Relation of each product or service to others in a competitor's line
- Production capacity utilization of competitors

Your Marketing Objectives

If market demand, real costs, customer value, and competition are accurately assessed, the resulting strategic price levels should maximize profits. All factors should be weighed against your organization's marketing objectives, however. You need to assess the impact of these factors upon

- Your other products or services
- Your need for short-term profits versus the importance of your long-term market position
- Skimming versus penetration objectives for a new product or service
- Long-term customer relations
- The importance of managing profits over the entire business cycle

You should never set prices in isolation from other considerations. Long-term marketing objectives may demand a short-term sacrifice of economic advantages that could be obtained through pricing. If a recession induces a price-cost squeeze, you might want to cut prices to your biggest customers, who may be suffering heavy losses. Maintaining margins in the short term might be much less important than retaining key customers' goodwill and solidifying your preferred-supplier position.

You might introduce a new product or service at a price level in line with your other offerings, even though a lower price would mean an immediate boost in volume and profits. Rather than go for big gains in one product or service area at the risk of cannibalizing your other products, you might decide that your first priority must be to protect the position of all your products or services.

When establishing price levels for each product or service and each customer or market segment, you should take into account the marketing objectives for your entire line and all your customers and market segments. Strategic pricing should be the cornerstone of your pricing policies. The key is advance planning rather than reacting to competitive moves.

Policies

Policies are rules to be observed under stated conditions. Policies are directives to subordinates and are intended to improve the validity of decisions and to achieve consistency of action among members of your organization. They should embody the best ideas in your organization and should be based on considerable experience. They should have been tested and found to be effective.

Policies make it unnecessary for your managers to think through each problem by giving them the benefit of many other peoples' experiences. Policies should reduce the number of poor decisions made. The following are some examples of pricing policies:

- Product quality shall be emphasized in all advertising, and price shall never be mentioned.

- Customers who are likely to be price-cutters are not to be sold to, if possible.

- No secret price-cutting or preferential treatment to customers will be practiced.

- Lost customers shall be called on and offered special purchase incentives.

- At least two items in the product line should be sold at the same price.

- Every competitive price change shall be met promptly.

- Price changes shall be announced at least one week before becoming effective.

See Fig. 2.2 for examples of pricing policies.

A. Alternative Price Level
1. Same as the competition
2. Lower than the competition
3. Higher than the competition

B. Alternative Price Flexibility
1. Single Price: all buyers pay one price, regardless of the quantity
2. Quantity Price: the price may vary with quantity, but all buyers of one quantity pay the same price
3. Flexible price: different buyers of one quantity may pay different prices

C. Alternative Introductory Price
1. Skimming: charge a low price to get buyers to try your product or service

D. Alternative Discounts and Allowances
1. Trade or Functional Discounts: for buyers who resell the product
2. Quantity Discounts: for large-quantity purchases
3. Cash Discounts: to buyers who pay within a specified time period
4. Seasonal Discounts: to buyers who purchase during the off-season
5. Trade-in Allowances: for trade-in of used products
6. Advertising Allowances: to resellers for advertising the product

E. Alternative Transportation Costs
1. FOB Pricing: adjust the price the buyer pays based on distribution costs
2. Uniform Delivered Pricing: buyers are charged the same price regardless of the location
3. Zone Pricing: all buyers within a geographic area pay one price
4. Freight Absorption Pricing: meet competitive prices by absorbing all or part of the actual transportation costs

Figure 2.2. Pricing policies — examples.

Tactical Pricing

Given a carefully thought out strategy, skillful strategic pricing can gain for you a significant competitive advantage, but it is not the sole route to substantial profit improvement. Don't overlook the power of effective tactical, or day-to-day, pricing. Many pricing battles have been won by employing adroit tactics. Some illustrative price-setting methods include the following:

- Add a target margin of profit to cost and compare the result with competitive prices.

- Take invoice cost (disregarding discounts) and add a given markup on invoice cost to arrive at a price.

- Charge a certain percentage less than a particular competitor.

- Take standard costs at a certain percent of capacity and add a specified margin to arrive at a price.

- Include items in your product or service line separated from each other by price differentials.

Two main considerations in tactical pricing are the timing and the amount of price changes. It is usually best to raise prices no more often than, say, once a year, so that your customers can depend on predictable prices for their own costing and pricing. The supplier who offers a stable price for a stated period is often the volume winner.

Remember that during economic squeezes, when you may be hesitant to increase your prices, your competitors may well welcome a price rise. If your rivals fail to follow an increase, the increase can be canceled or selectively withdrawn by offering discounts to key customers while maximizing margins in less sensitive areas. Selectivity is often a very good idea. One question to answer when considering price changes is when should you play the role of price leader. In all cases, price moves should be carefully considered in advance to avoid the quick reactions that often limit profits or market share.

Shrewd management of price changes is a key to tactical success in pricing. Many gains made here can be negated, however, if your authority system for day-to-day price quoting is not consistent with the revenue and cost economics of your product or service line. Optimally, the person making tactical price decisions should have access to information regarding

- Costs (including order-specific and customer-specific costs)
- Price objectives based on profit targets
- Which suppliers have won and lost in attempting to sell to key customers and market segments (and at what prices)
- Most recent prices paid by key customers and market segments
- Current competitive price levels

Armed with this information, you or your price setter will be in a position to set the best price based on tradeoffs between

- Overall market prices
- Customer-specific price levels

- Profitability
- Your profit objectives

The Value of Price Planning

This discussion has dealt with the various planning dimensions of setting prices. Some or all of the strategies described may be useful; however, some may be dispensable or even counterproductive if improperly managed.

Organizations invariably benefit from having intelligently and wisely formulated objectives, strategies, policies, and tactics. But ill-conceived predetermined pricing rules can be harmful. If management will not or cannot take the time to develop valid and useful price rules, it may be wise to allow an organization's executives to make pricing decisions on an ad hoc basis.

The value of planning to an organization depends largely upon the caliber of executives and managers at various levels. Organizations with great executive strength at the top and relative weakness below gain most from well-devised objectives, strategies, policies, and tactics.

Executives who specialize in an area of decision making should ordinarily participate in the formulation and evaluation of alternatives. This way they can learn the rationale behind the rules, constraints, guides, policies, and tactics in case they need to apply them to circumstances to which they were not originally intended to apply. Rules may need to be relaxed and revised as circumstances change. Organizations operating in volatile, complex environments must not set down rigid rules and constraints that can quickly become inappropriate or ineffective as conditions change.

Top managers who do not formulate clear objectives, policies, and strategies and who do not decide how particular decisions will be made must take measures to ensure that their directives are communicated to and understood by subordinates. It should be clear what executives understand the organization's rules to be. Faulty communications can be hazardous for an organization.*

Selecting a Price Strategy

How do you go about selecting a price strategy? Actually, the alternatives for pricing are as diverse as the numbers of organizations setting prices, as changeable as the economic environment, and as volatile as competitor

---

*For a good, detailed coverage of price planning, see Oxenfeldt, the major reference for this chapter. Other references used include Kotler, Bell, and Guiltinan and Paul.

and customer reactions. Here we hope to demonstrate how you can use a systematic, logical approach for choosing a pricing strategy.

Skim Pricing.   Skim pricing refers to pricing products or services at very high levels to skim the "cream" of the profits off the market. You might use this strategy when

- There is little danger of short-term competition (due to patent control, high market-entry costs, new technology)
- Product uniqueness creates relatively price-insensitive demand
- Demand must be limited until production is geared up
- Organization policy demands recovering start-up costs rapidly

When you consider a skim pricing strategy, consider how your end user will perceive your product or service. Make sure that your prospective customers are willing to pay a high price.

Slide-Down Pricing.   A modification of the skim pricing strategy is the slide-down strategy of moving prices downward over time. This usually follows a skim pricing strategy as the product or service becomes more appealing to a larger group of potential buyers. The price is periodically lowered to penetrate more of the market, and competitors are often discouraged from entering the market.

Penetration Pricing.   This strategy refers to pricing products or services low in order to gain entry into a market or to increase existing market share. This might be considered in order to

- Establish an initial market position rapidly
- Discourage new competitors from entering the market
- Take advantage of competitors who will not react to lower prices
- Go for maximum market share and return on investment

Elasticity Pricing.   To use this strategy, price products or services high or low to take advantage of known or perceived price sensitivity of the customer or market segment. This might be used when

- The market will likely respond to lower prices with a much higher purchase volume
- The market will likely respond to high prices with little or no reduction in purchase volume

If the product or service is promoted heavily on value, customers may be willing to pay high prices for this value.

Follow Pricing.   To employ the strategy of follow pricing, you price products with respect to industry price leaders. You must be on the alert for competitive price changes. Consider this strategy when

- Your organization is small and your industry is dominated by a few competitors with major market shares
- Industry price leaders would react to unusually high or low prices
- A product or service is undifferentiated from others available

Segment Pricing.   Segment pricing refers to pricing the same products differently in different markets, perhaps using different product or service strategies. This strategy is important when buyers are different enough to buy at different prices for slight product or service differences. Assuming that it is legal in a particular instance, segment pricing allows market segment scanning for available niches. This strategy might be used when

- A product or service is useful to different market segments
- A product or service can be altered to meet the requirements of various segments
- Different market segments do not compete

Cost-Plus Pricing.   You build a price from the cost floor up with this strategy. The emphasis here is on the way that one cost is added to a profit target to obtain a price. This strategy is not as flexible as market-oriented ones but might be used when

- The product or service is sold in a government market
- Total costs are unpredictable
- A new product is being tested

Flexible Pricing.   With this pricing strategy, you price products or services to meet competitive or marketplace conditions as these conditions change. This strategy is followed when

- There is an important competitive challenge
- Competitors attack with penetration pricing
- Demand levels are changing

Preemptive Pricing.   This strategy involves pricing products or services to discourage competitive market entry. Preemptive pricing is used as an early line of defense to protect a dominant market position. This strategy could be used to

- Support a strong market position and keep competitors out of the market
- Satisfy market needs through price, product or service, and promotion to gain brand loyalty

Phaseout Pricing.   To use this strategy, price products or services high while removing them from the line. "Milk" or "harvest" a product by keeping the product available but keep the sales profitable by using high prices. Use this strategy when

A. Core Pricing Approaches

   1. Price low to keep competitors out and maintain market share.
   2. Meet competitors head-on.
   3. Maintain dollar percentage above or below the competition.
   4. Price according to estimated market value.

B. High Price Strategies

   1. Use when
      a. You need to preserve a quality image.
      b. Demand exceeds supply.
      c. You have monopolistic control.

   2. You must
      a. Have a high quality product.
      b. Stand behind your product.
      c. Have control over distribution.
      d. Be a guarantee leader.

C. Moderate Price Strategies

   1. Price close to the industry level.
   2. Hold your current market position.
   3. Have a strong tracking and response system.

D. Low Price Strategies

   1. Increase your short-run volume and market share.
   2. Hold a least-cost position and have the ability to hold fast.

Figure 2.3. Pricing strategies—examples.

- A product or service is still used but demand is falling in the long run
- Customers can easily obtain a similar product or service
- A product or service line must be trimmed down to a more manageable size

Loss Leader Pricing. You are using the strategy of loss leader pricing when you price low to attract buyers for other products or services. This is often used when

- A seller wishes to build customer traffic
- Complement products are available to be sold at higher prices with the loss leader item

Summary of Pricing Strategies

Selecting the right pricing strategy is a basic part of the pricing process. Most price strategies can be used in combinations so that overall pricing strategy can be fitted to your needs. Whatever pricing strategy you choose, it cannot be isolated from your total marketing and production mix. (See Fig. 2.3 for a summary of pricing strategies.)*

*See Oxenfeldt for a good in-depth coverage of pricing strategy.

3

Setting Prices for New Products and Services

Introduction

By studying demand and cost at various price levels, it is possible to select an optimum price for a new product or service. Two pricing strategies for new products are skim pricing and penetration pricing. The guiding force behind your pricing decisions should be your pricing objectives, either market-oriented or cost-oriented.

Few organizations can afford to be indifferent toward cost in approaching new product or service pricing. Setting prices always involves unknown reactions of customers and competitors to price, and this uncertainty increases for new products or services.

In setting the initial price for a new product or service, you should consider

- Relevant market segments
- Diversity of customer or user demands
- Impact of price upon competitive actions
- Cost considerations
- Marketing channel strategies

You must account for your unit costs and sales of your other products or services. Given the many variables to be considered and the uncertain impact of price on each element singly and in combination, you definitely need a systematic means for setting the initial price. You need an orderly procedure for new products and services even more than you do for existing ones. See Fig. 3.1 for an overview of this process. Assuming that you know what your new product or service will cost, should you add a markup for profit and let that be the price? Should you guess at what your product is worth versus what the competition's product is worth? Should you survey customers or users to see what they would be willing to pay?

A. Identify your target consumer or user prospects and their needs:
   1. Design a system to serve market segments separately.
   2. Determine margins and special costs of each segment.

B. Describe your segment environments and decide how to reach these segments:
   1. Define customer or user support required.
   2. Determine price ranges to offer.
   3. Determine price and/or feature differences among offerings.

C. Profile your probable competitors:
   1. Identify likely competitive prices.
   2. Identify competitive strengths.

D. Identify price alternatives:
   1. Estimate sales at desired price levels and timing.
   2. Estimate direct product or service costs.
   3. Identify differences in costs of product or service changes.

E. Estimate direct and indirect production and marketing costs at different levels of sales volume.

F. Calculate expected profit at different levels of sales volume for each market segment:
   1. Account for real and perceived quality differences among competitive products.
   2. Drop items that will not provide adequate profit.

G. Establish price differentials among your products or services: make sure that item sales will cover product or service line costs directly or by stimulating sales of other products or services.

H. Explore effects of price changes and determine the most advantageous prices for different market situations.

Figure 3.1. Setting a price—a systematic approach.

Markup or Cost-Plus Pricing.   Pricing questions do not always have clear-cut answers. The markup or cost-plus method of pricing is popular and has the advantage that it aims not only to recover the product or service costs but also to generate a profit. It does not address the question of what price the market is willing to pay. Its lack of flexibility and sensitivity to market factors is a major drawback that may make adjustments necessary if the product or service does not sell well.

Market-Oriented Pricing.   This method of pricing can be either demand-oriented or competition-oriented. Customers or users will often infer quality from price. If you price higher than the competition, you may assume that consumers or users will decide that your product or service is better and have an incentive to buy from you. Alternatively, consumers or users may perceive your offering to have the same or lower value than competitive offerings and therefore consider your product or service to be overpriced. Or buyers may compare your prices with other offerings and decide to buy what you offer because they view your product or service as unique, allowing you to price it higher.

Surveying consumers or users may not give you an accurate representation of buying situations. How do you decide on the best way to price a new product or service? Two very different strategies are classic for new product or service pricing: skim pricing and penetration pricing.

Skim Pricing Considerations

High initial price is well suited to a dramatically different product or service — one that creates an entirely new market. An innovative product or service is not familiar and a consumer or user cannot easily judge the value. Demand stimulation via low price will not likely be very effective at first. Initially, market resistance may be high and few prospective buyers may want to take a chance. For those who do buy, high price may not be an important deterrent to purchase and in some cases may even encourage purchase of an "exclusive" product. As the product or service becomes well known, buyer responsiveness to price often can increase substantially.

If you were to use slide-down pricing in the same situation, charging several different prices in sequence, you might increase revenues and profits significantly. You would start high and drop prices as market acceptance increased. Any price differentiation among market segments must be isolated to prevent arbitrage, which is buyer switching from high-priced to low-priced products. With a sequence of slide-down prices, there is always only one prevailing price.

When price reductions are too frequent or too predictable, people who would pay a high price may wait until the price falls before they buy. Try to use only a few price reductions.

Some reasons for using skim pricing include the following:

- R & D and market commercialization costs can be recouped before competitive pressures drive prices downward.
- Long-term cash outlays represent high cost.
- You have some protection from competitive imitation and market invasion.
- You want to feel out the market without extensive test marketing.
- You want to establish a quality image for your product or service.
- You want your prices to reflect current production and distribution costs at limited levels of output.

Skim pricing enables you to lower your costs and prices through economies of scale and possibly the experience curve. Perhaps you can't satisfy demand at a low initial price but you can use high initial prices to manage demand fulfillment.

Penetration Pricing Considerations

Since success with penetration pricing demands high unit sales volume, your product or service must be one that appeals to a large number of people. Penetration pricing makes your product or service affordable to a large market, allowing you to achieve high volume and market share.

Skim pricing charges the maximum the market will allow, gaining a sizable profit from low volume (contribution margin is high). Conversely, penetration pricing keeps profit per unit low and depends on high-quantity sales to generate profit. If the potential market is large, this can be an effective strategy. High price is appropriate if market potential is limited. Otherwise, you are quite vulnerable. Low price discourages competition and sets up a market entry barrier by requiring large-scale investments to undercut prices. Penetration pricing can give you substantial rewards, establishing you firmly in your markets.

A low, stable price strategy is likely to create for you brand loyalty and repeat buying. This strategy is aggressive but appropriate when your product or service distinctiveness is low and competitive entry and growth is likely.*

*See Bell, Chapter 17.

Adapting Pricing Approaches to Your Needs

In Chapter 5 of his book *Pricing Strategies and Practices,* Norton Paley discusses the following ways that skim pricing can be adapted to different situations to fit your needs:

- *A double approach.* Use both skim pricing and penetration pricing together. If various market segments differ in price elasticity, it may be best to apply both strategies simultaneously in different parts of the market.

- *A concurrent application.* Use skim pricing in many areas at the same time for the same product or service but at different prices.

- *A distribution and functional differentiation.* Use skimming to sell products or services at higher prices for qualitative or quantitative reasons. Sell to wholesalers at different prices than to direct retail accounts.

- *An extreme concurrent application.* Use skim pricing in price-insensitive (low-elasticity) market sectors and penetration pricing in price-sensitive (high-elasticity) sectors of the market.

Keep in mind that the price of your product or service will probably affect (and be affected by) other products or services. A high-price policy may rub off on other products in the form of a quality or luxury image, and a low-price policy might help sell other items by conveying the image of good value for the price. Carefully study such possibilities before arriving at a final price.

Avoid pricing low for easy market entry while counting on raising prices after you gain market share. The low introductory price creates a price and value relationship in the buyers' minds that is very difficult to alter. Another danger is to overlook inflation by entering the market at prices based on current costs. Try to anticipate cost increases for the foreseeable future and build them into your price structure from the beginning.

Review Pricing Factors

To select the best approach to pricing, consider these guidelines set forth by Paley:

- *Advertising budget.* If your promotional budget is low, a low price must "do the talking," while a high price allows you more promotional spending.

- *Product type.* A commodity-type product offered by many competitors has to be price-competitive. A unique, patented item can be premium-priced.

- *Mode of manufacture.* The degree of market coverage affects price levels. Intensive distribution causes (and is the result of) lower prices. Low prices get you more widespread coverage with resulting economies of scale and lower allowable prices. Selective coverage, used as an inducement to resellers to try harder, usually means higher prices.

- *Product obsolescence.* If a product will be viable for a long life span, its price can be lower because costs will be spread over several years. If product life is short, charge a high price and "milk" the product.

- *Technological change.* Prices and changes in technology often move together. Technological innovation often offers more convenience or better performance, so customers may feel a technologically advanced item is worth a higher price. Or if technological changes result in lower supplier cost, prices in the market could be lowered.

- *Production emphasis.* If production is highly mechanized or automated, resulting savings can lead to lower prices. Gains with automated production may be higher than are possible with labor-intensive production.

- *Market-share goal.* Market share and price usually move in opposite directions — a higher share desired means a lower price must be offered. If a low market share is acceptable or the only share possible, demand can be controlled by high price.

- *Marketing channels.* The number of levels in your marketing channels will affect price. With more levels come higher prices to marketing intermediaries for reselling the product.

- *Stage of market.* Pricing policies vary over the market life of a product. High prices are used in both the introductory and declining stages of a product or service. In the introductory stage, buyers have only limited ability to compare and evaluate prices, and they will tend to be price-insensitive. During product or service decline, shrinking sales volume and increased costs put upward pressure on prices.

- *Profit perspective.* Profit goals will influence the choice of a price policy. For early payback, prices are set high. To build steady long-term sales, prices are kept low.

- *Product versatility.* The range of product or service applications affects price. A multipurpose product usually can command a higher price than a single-use item.

- *Effect on other products.* A new product or service may be so important to rounding out your product or service line that you choose penetration

Product or project: Radio		
Planning period: 1985		
Tax rate: 45%		
Gross margin required: 40%		
After-tax ROI: 12.5%		
Total investment required: $300,000		

After-tax ROI		$ 37,500
Taxes @ 45%		30,682
Pretax profit required		68,182
Assignable period expenses:		
Production	$200,000	
Administration	30,000	
Selling	50,000	
Promotion	100,000	
Total period expenses		380,000
Gross profit		448,182
Cost of goods or services		672,273
Sales dollars required		$1,120,455
Sales forecast		30,000 units
Price/unit required		$ 37.35

Figure 3.2. Pricing analysis: target ROI.

pricing to increase sales of your more profitable items. A price should not be viewed in isolation, but for its overall product-line effects and profit contribution.

- *Ancillary services.* Build into a package price the cost of ancillary services such as installation or user training.

- *Product life in use.* A product of lasting value justifies a higher price than a throwaway item.

- *Turnover.* Slow-moving items require a higher markup than faster-selling items.

- *Price differentiation.* This is an active marketing tool that is not used under a penetration policy but rather within a skimming framework.

- *Amortization of investment.* Pay back invested money quickly with a high price, slowly with a low price.

- *Threat of competitive entry.* Prefer a low-price policy if a competitive threat exists. If no threat exists, choose skimming.

- *Sales objective.* If your sales objective is one of gradual market expansion, choose skim pricing. To maximize early sales volume, choose penetration pricing.

Use the above criteria to assist you in choosing the best new product or

Product or project: Radio
Planning period: 1985
Proposed Price: $29.95
Forecasted unit sales: $55,000
Desired ROI: 13.5%
Total investment required: $655,000

Projected sales		$1,647,250
Less required markup:		
Selling expense	$178,000	
Administration expense	$ 43,000	
Profit required	$ 88,425	
Total markup		$ 309,425
Total production cost		$1,337,825
Production costs/units		$ 24.32

Figure 3.3. Pricing analysis: calculate production costs given forecasted sales and price.

service price strategy. New product or service pricing should begin early, with projected cost/price ratios guiding product or service development and market introduction. Carefully and continually monitor internal and external price-influencing factors to enable you to reprice in response to changing conditions. Figures 3.2 and 3.3 illustrate how the Price Plan pricing system can be used to locate a price given a target return on investment objective.

4

Product or Service Line Pricing

What should you do if you must set prices for a line of products or services? Such a line might be required to enable you to meet the diverse needs of your customers or users. To market a line of products or services to a particular market segment, price differentials must be established for each item in the line.

The price-differential amounts depend on differences in sales-volume expectations, costs, and product or service performance. High-cost, unusual, or high-performance products or services are priced high, while lower-cost, basic, or conventional products or services are priced lower. Your line might include a promotional item sold at less than its average total production cost in order to attract potential buyers. In some cases you or the actual seller of the product or service might encourage buyers to trade up to better-performing and higher-priced items.

You should make price-level decisions only after examining the effects of the price on the rest of your product or service line. Other products or services in your line may be substitute or complement items. When a price change on one item influences the sales volume of another item, some degree of cross-price elasticity of demand exists.

Cross-Price Elasticity of Demand, Substitutes, and Complements

The demand for a product or service X will usually depend not only on its own price, price (X), but upon prices of other items, such as price (Y). The definition of this relationship, known as cross-price elasticity of demand, is

$$\text{Cross-elasticity}(X,Y) = \frac{[\text{quantity}(X2) - \text{quantity}(X1)]/\text{quantity}(X1)}{[\text{price}(Y2) - \text{price}(Y1)]/\text{price}(Y1)}$$

$$= \frac{\text{change in quantity of } X}{\text{change in price of } Y} \times \frac{\text{price of } Y}{\text{quantity of } X}$$

The cross-elasticity can be either positive or negative. If it is positive, the two items are *substitutes*—a rise in the price of Y raises the consumption of X. If the cross-elasticity is negative, the items are *complements*—a rise in the price of Y lowers the consumption of X. (See Figs. 4.1 and 4.2a and b.)

Interrelated Demand — Substitutes

Substitutes are characterized by the fact that small changes in price ratios (with no change in real buyer income) will lead to large shifts in the relative quantities purchased. Complements are characterized by the fact that large changes in price ratios (with no change in real buyer income) will lead to only small shifts in the relative quantities purchased.

Substitutes exist when you market a line of products or services, each of which serves slightly different target market segments. If you offer items with varying quality levels or options, price differentials should reflect the relationship between price and value to the customer or user. These differentials should be large enough to represent distinct alternatives. Usually, price differentials should represent relative, rather than absolute, price differences.

As prices rise, the size of the price differential needed for a noticeable

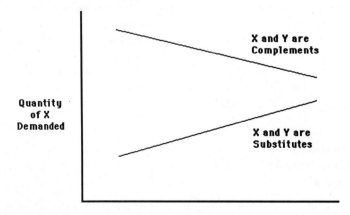

Price of Y

Figure 4.1. Interrelated product or service demand.

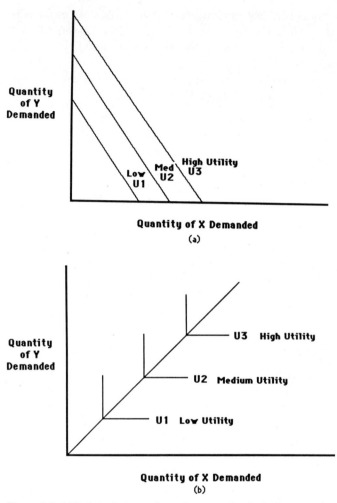

Figure 4.2. (a) Perfect substitutes: demand at various levels of utility; (b) perfect complements: demand at various levels of utility.

price difference increases. Select the minimum differential needed to em- phasize quality differences, and find the percentage increase over your lowest-priced item that provides a just-noticeable price difference. Use this percentage for setting other minimum differentials.

You may also be interested in getting buyers to trade up within your line. If price differentials are too large, you might not succeed. By selecting minimum differentials needed to recover costs and to emphasize quality differences, you could encourage buyers to consider the next-higher- priced item.

When you make price changes to stimulate sales of one item in your line, you should consider possible substitution effects. If the price of one item in your line is cut, sales will likely increase. However, sales of your similar items may suffer as buyers substitute these items. You should know which market segments are most likely to respond to a price change, and you should be sure to estimate the effect of lost sales on your other products or services when you evaluate price change effects.

Interrelated Demand — Complements

Complements are product or service items that increase in sales volume when related items are reduced in price. Oxenfeldt (1975) points out the following reasons for this:

1. *Related value.*   When two products or services are used in conjunction with one another, purchase of one item may lead to purchase of the second. For example, men's suits are purchased with men's ties; computers are purchased with printers.

2. *Enhanced value.*   One product or service may enhance the value or increase the utilization of another. A camera attachment makes the camera easier and more interesting to use.

3. *Quality supplements.*   Items designed for repair, maintenance, or operating assistance may enable a buyer to obtain (or maintain) a high level of quality performance. Service contracts sold with electronic products are very much in demand.

4. *Broader assortments.*   Products or services totally unrelated in use may be complementary if bought from the same source. Shopping at only one store reduces the buyer's search costs.

Analyzing cross-price elasticity of demand for complementary product or service items is often difficult. Guiltinan and Paul suggest that you could capitalize upon complementary relationships via the leader and bundling methods.

The *leader* method employs a high-margin strategy on complementary items when demand for one item is elastic. (This is effective only where there is incentive to purchase from a single source because of, for example, compatibility, convenience, or prestige.)

Bundling involves offering special prices to buyers purchasing the main items plus one or more auxiliary items. This is widely used in industrial marketing when complementary products and services exist. In order to be effective, bundling requires that true complementary relationships exist.

Interrelated Costs

Two items are interrelated in cost when a change in the production of one affects the cost of the other. By-products and joint products are examples of related items. If the production of ham is cut down, the production of pork will be also. The unit cost of the pork will then rise because the overhead is spread over fewer units.

Any two products or services using the same production facilities are interrelated in cost even if they are not joint products. If a seller increases the price of one product or service and causes sales to fall, the cost of other products or services will be higher (assuming they are not complements). You must examine cost interactions before changing prices in your line. See Figs. 4.3a and b. (Also see the PricePlan CVP Breakeven Analysis: Product Combinations worksheet program. Examples appear in Figs. 4.4a and b.)

Price Determination
by Cost Base

Costs provide a good starting point for determining prices of interrelated items in a product or service line. Although there is disagreement over which costs to use, the three most popular cost bases are full costs, incremental costs, and conversion costs.

Suppose you offer two types of specialty product or service item. One requires more labor but less material cost per unit than the other. The approaches to price determination, using the three cost bases, are to

Set prices proportional to full costs. If both products or services have the same full costs, they bear the same price. The allocation of overhead sometimes involves arbitrary assignments of costs, so resulting prices may be somewhat arbitrary as well. You may be blind to profit opportunities if prices of both items are not geared to the recovery of the arbitrary overhead costs.

Set prices proportional to incremental costs. You charge buyers in proportion to the extra costs incurred in supplying additional units of the product or service. Supplying an additional unit of one item results in less additional cost than would supplying another unit of the other item. The net effect is to shift sales toward the product or service that absorbs more overhead.

Set prices proportional to conversion costs. Conversion costs are the labor and overhead required to convert purchased materials into finished products or services. The value added to your product or service is found by subtracting purchased material costs from allocated full costs.

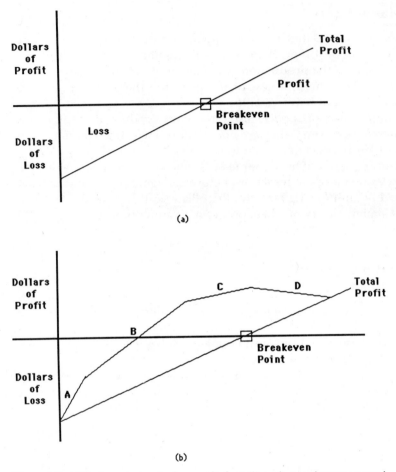

Figure 4.3. (a) Single-product cost-volume-profit chart; (b) product-combinations cost-volume-profit chart.

The idea is that profits should be based on the value added to each unit, and the effect on price is to shift sales toward items having more material cost. Scarce resources, such as labor and machines, are thus economized.

Incremental costs normally provide a lower limit to individual product or service item pricing, but a uniform markup over incremental or other costs is deceiving in that it ignores different demand intensities, cross-elasticities, competitive conditions, and life cycle characteristics of each product or service.

Your overall goal in setting product or service line prices is to improve the marketability and profitability of your entire line. To be competitive,

Product or projects: KM
Planning period: 1985
Group fixed costs: $7,500

Product (Project)				Average contribution margin	Sales			Contribution	
#	Name	Price/unit	Direct costs/unit		Units	Dollars	% $ Total	Product*	% of group
1	Radio	$45.95	$31.84	.31	4,500	$206,775	26.3	63,495	23
2	Stereo	69.95	45.33	.35	6,300	440,685	56	155,106	56.1
3	Records	39.95	23.42	.41	3,500	139,825	17.8	57,855	20.9
	Totals			.35	14,300	$787,285	100.0	276,456	100.0

*(Price/unit − direct costs/unit) × units.

Product or project: KM
Planning period: 1985
Group fixed costs: $7,500

KM group summary:

Sales	$787,285
Direct costs	510,829
Contribution	276,456
Fixed costs	7,500
Profit before tax	268,956
Tax @ 45%	121,030
Profit after tax	147,926
Breakeven dollars	21,358
Margin of safety	97.29%
Operating leverage	1.03

Figure 4.4. Cost-volume-profit analysis: product combinations.

to satisfy customer or user requirements, and to meet the demands of resellers, you may need to compromise by lowering price or offering more product or service at the same price. A common pricing method known as *price lining* is used when a seller selects a set of price differentials which are applied to all items sold. Each product or price in a line is priced relative to other items in the line to form distinct price bands.

When retailers and wholesalers use price lining, manufacturers must set prices accordingly. To market profitably at these levels, manufacturers must carefully control design features and manufacturing costs. The pressure from consumers and the trade dictates which pricing alternatives are open to manufacturers.

Discount Structures (Price Adjustments)

Discounts (and extras, or premiums), which are established to adjust for variations in product or service offerings; customer or user requirements; and offerings by the competition, constitute the pricing structure, i.e., the actual price offered to prospective buyers in the marketplace. Discounts and extras can be designed to fit a variety of pricing situations:

Trade (functional) discounts. These discounts are often granted on the basis of a customer's position in the industry marketing-channel system (retailer, jobber, distributor, or manufacturer). Trade discounts reflect typical customer cost and profit levels.

Quantity discounts. A seller may accept lower unit prices for items sold in large quantities than for items sold in small lots. A cumulative discount is based on the total amount of business with a customer over time and is calculated on expected sales volume or past experience. A noncumulative discount is based on the quantity included with a particular order only.

Promotional allowances. These allowances take two forms, permanent or special. Permanent schedules of allowances are often set up with resellers for performing promotional activities. A cooperative advertising program might be established to encourage resellers to advertise a manufacturer's products. A special promotional allowance is a short-term allowance related to a particular campaign. To build up retail stocks before a large-scale promotion, a manufacturer might offer a special promotional incentive to retailers, for example, a direct discount or free goods.

Locational discounts. The cost of moving a product from manufacturer to customer must be recovered in order for the transaction to be profitable. FOB pricing, uniform delivered pricing, zone pricing, and unsystematic freight equalization and methods for recovering or absorbing moving costs.

FOB (free on board) pricing adds the cost of transportation to the manufacturer's selling price to determine delivered cost to the customer. FOB pricing is difficult to administer if you have a broad line and wide geographical customer dispersion.

With FOB pricing, customers expect manufacturers to ship merchandise by the most economical method. Therefore, this pricing method can place certain sellers at a price disadvantage compared to competitors located closer to a customer.

Uniform delivered pricing involves charging the same delivered price to each customer. This is often used when selling products for which transportation costs are low relative to the value of goods. It may also be used when a single price is advertised throughout the country.

Zone pricing is used when transportation costs are large in relation to the value of goods. It is similar to uniform delivered pricing in that customers within a zone all pay the same price, but delivered prices differ from one zone to the next.

Unsystematic freight equalization occurs when you meet competitors' delivered prices in order to maintain market share. Sellers offer locational discounts to particular customers through absorption of freight costs. This pricing method is feasible in the long run only when incremental profit from added business more than offsets the costs of freight absorption.

Terms of payment. Arrangements for payment are usually classified as cash or time-payment discounts. To induce prompt payment, a cash discount may be offered, providing a specific percentage reduction for prompt payment and stipulating the period of time over which payment must be made. Many variations can be offered. For example, for seasonal merchandise, invoices may be dated so payment is not required until the buyer's selling season begins.

Quoting prices. To translate basic prices, discounts, and extras into actual selling prices, a list price for each item is often used. The list price might be identical to a base price or adjusted downward from the base price. It is easier and quicker to change the discount structure than to change list prices. Different discount sheets can be distributed to different customer groups without raising questions or concern about discrimination.

To quote prices, a seller begins with the list price and then deducts each discount. Trade discounts are deducted, and then quantity, promotional, and cash discounts are usually taken. Transportation costs are added to the list price minus discounts to arrive at the final quoted price.*

* See Bell, Chapter 8.

5

Changing Prices and Pricing Under Uncertainty

The usefulness of any pricing program depends upon understanding the impact of changing prices on the demand for a product or service. Price changes can affect unit sales volume and revenue per unit.

Price Elasticity of Demand

Price elasticity of demand is an important concept in price planning. If a change in price causes a change in unit sales volume, then demand is price-sensitive. More important, though, is the possible effect on total revenue.

Price elasticity of demand is measured by the percentage change in quantity divided by the percentage change in price. If P_1 represents the initial price and Q_1 represents the initial quantity demanded, the elasticity of a change in price, P_2, is represented by

$$\text{Arc price elasticity of demand } e = \frac{(Q_2 - Q_1)/[(Q_2 + Q_2)/2]}{(P_2 - P_1)/[(P_2 + P_1)/2]}$$

When e can be calculated, the impact of price changes on revenue can be predicted.

If elasticity is -1 or less (more negative), demand is very sensitive to price, and the change in revenue will be in the direction opposite that of the price change. If elasticity is greater (more positive) than -1, demand is not price-sensitive, and the increase (or decrease) in price will cause a smaller increase (or decrease) in revenue.

In practice, it is difficult to develop a numerically precise indicator of elasticity. However, being able to determine whether e is greater than -1 or less than -1 will enable you to understand the general impact of a price change on revenue and profit. See Figs. 5.1 and 5.2 for graphic examples of this.

Market versus Organization (or Product or Service) Elasticity

Market elasticity indicates how demand responds to change in average prices of all competitors. Organization (or product or service) elasticity indicates the willingness of existing buyers to switch suppliers or of new buyers to choose a supplier based on price. For a product like table salt, market demand is inelastic because people cannot consume much more salt, even if all prices are lowered. If only one producer lowers price, that producer will gain market share. Even though market demand may be inelastic, organization (or product or service) demand can be elastic because buyers may be very sensitive to competitive price differences.

Even during elastic demand periods, some products or services can experience inelastic organization demand if they are clearly differentiated with respect to quality. During inelastic periods of market demand, organi-

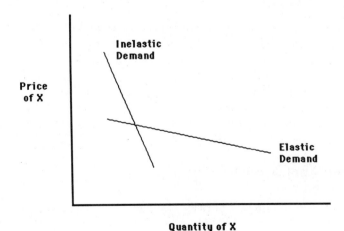

Figure 5.1. Price elasticity of demand: elastic versus inelastic demand.

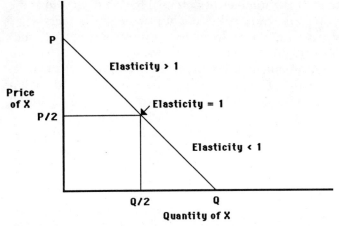

Figure 5.2. Price elasticity of demand: linear demand curve.

zation (or product or service) demand can be elastic if price is important to buyers in selecting a specific product or service. Primary demand—for the generic product type—can be stimulated by price only if market demand is elastic. Selective demand—for a specific product or service offering (such as a specific brand)—can be stimulated by price only if the organization (or product or service) demand is elastic.

Factors in the Buying Process

You can gain many insights into the price elasticity of market and organization (or product or service) demand by examining buying process factors that suggest that market demand might be elastic, such as the following:

1. Many alternative offerings (substitutes) exist.
2. Only a small percentage of prospective buyers actually own or purchase the product or service, because of price.
3. The price represents a high percentage of buyer income or budget for purchases.
4. Rates of consumption or replacement can be increased with low prices.
5. Reseller or manufacturer demand is price-elastic—if the price is lowered, the reseller or manufacturer can lower prices on the final product, and demand increases.

If an industrywide price decline results in increased customer willingness or ability to purchase, the gap between market potential and industry sales becomes smaller. Price will have an impact on demand for a product or service if other items have similar performance characteristics, allowing substitution to occur. If the number of potential buyers is far above the number of current buyers, lower prices might gain new customers.

Elasticity will be greater if buyers do not have strong supplier (or brand) preferences. In some situations, perceived differences in quality will not exist and perceived economic risk will be high relative to performance, convenience, or other risk. Price then will probably be a potentially important buying factor. If the cost of finding substitutes is low, demand will likely be elastic.

In most markets, demand will be elastic in some market segments and inelastic in others. You should examine buying process factors in the largest market segments you select (or consider for selection) in your marketing strategy. Consider the following factors before you attempt to estimate price elasticity.

1. A price change will have no effect unless it is large enough to be noticeable.

2. A price set too low brings questions about quality.

3. Buyer price expectations are not exact, only approximate.

4. Price judgments are made about expected prices at each quality level.

Competition

Competitor reactions to price changes must be considered. If all competitors match price changes, it is probable no market share gains will result. Price changes will have no effect unless industry price levels affect primary demand. You should try to determine what your competitors' reactions will be to your price changes.

If you are considering a price reduction, competitors may match the reduction if market demand is elastic. However, if product or service demand is already close to the market potential, competitors may react only if they believe that demand for their product or service offerings is elastic. If you consider a price increase, expect competitors to follow if they believe that their product or service offerings have inelastic demands.

Examine historical competitor behaviors. Some competitors base prices on costs, pricing either very aggressively (to capitalize upon cost advantages) or very conservatively (to avoid getting into price wars). You might be able to gain insights into probable buyer reactions. If an industry has experienced extensive price cutting, buyers will more likely be price-sensitive from experience.

Determinants of Demand

Why is the demand for some products and services great and that for others small? Why are products and services which are necessities demanded relatively more by poor people and products and services which are considered luxuries demanded relatively more by rich people? Very poor people must concentrate on meeting their basic physiological needs, and rich people can afford to indulge in aesthetic products and services and those products and services that provide social distinction.

For novel products and services, there is usually an initial penetration phase during which an item is still new and demand is affected by the learning process. This penetration phase tends to be followed by a replacement phase after market saturation is reached.

We know that individual responsiveness to price can be measured by the price elasticity of demand:

$$e = \frac{\text{change in quantity of } X}{\text{change in price of } X} \times \frac{\text{price of } X}{\text{quantity of } X}$$

What are the determinants of individual buyer demand?

1. *Closeness of substitutes.* Demand for a product or service will tend to be more elastic the more numerous and the closer are the available substitutes.

2. *Luxuries versus necessities.* Demand for a luxury product or service will be more elastic than demand for a necessity item. (A luxury is taken here to be a strongly superior product or service which is much more heavily purchased as buyer income rises. A necessity is a product or service almost as much of which is consumed at low as at high buyer income.)

3. *Importance of the product or service.* If a product or service is important (if its purchase accounts for a large fraction of the buyer's budget), it tends to have elastic demand.

4. *High-priced versus low-priced products and services.* High-priced products and services tend to have elastic demands and low-priced items inelastic demands. A high price is one for which a buyer's desired quantity approaches zero.

Estimating Price Elasticity of Demand

Your ability to achieve your price objectives depends upon price elasticity of demand for your product or service offerings. Several methods exist for estimating elasticities.

Statistical Estimation. Historical information may exist that indicates the effects of changes in a marketing variable on sales revenues. You can use statistical methods (such as simple or multiple linear and nonlinear regression models) to examine relationships between marketing variables and price. (See planning tools from KM Software Solutions for help here.)

Statistical methods will not always be feasible. Competitors' prices are needed, and factors other than price may affect sales. It is difficult to separate such effects from price effects, even if data on all factors are available.

Experiments. Experiments in which actual retail prices are manipulated (holding other factors constant) are sometimes used to examine the effects of price on sales. This can be useful, but it can also be costly and time-consuming. Your competitors often will know what you are doing, and they may alter their price strategies to confuse your results. Another possible drawback is that you may not get cooperation from distributors or retailers.

Laboratory experiments can be useful, too, in which you vary prices in a simulated market environment. This allows great control over price, because all prices can be manipulated at once. Lack of realism is a problem, however.

Customer or User Surveys. Direct customer or user research can be used to estimate price elasticity, especially when determining acceptable price ranges. Prospective buyers may be asked what they would be willing to pay for the product or service. This type of research is designed to estimate the degree of market elasticity, not numbers of buyers. Surveys can help to find the extent to which price will affect buying decisions.

Judgment. Statistical methods, experiments, and direct questioning can provide useful information, but you can also make use of judgment about effects of price changes. Knowledge of the buying process and of your competition can be extremely helpful in projecting price elasticity, even if other methods are used.

You can get measures of elasticity from estimates of unit demand (from either management opinion or market surveys) for each price being offered. Group the estimate in the following categories:

1. Optimistic — best case, low probability
2. Most likely — realistic case, high probability
3. Pessimistic — worst case, low probability

Using a beta distribution, you can calculate expected volume from these estimates:

$$\text{Expected volume} = \frac{\text{pessimistic} + (4 \times \text{most likely}) + \text{optimistic}}{6}$$

Assume, for a given price, these demand estimates:

Optimistic volume = 600 units
Most likely volume = 450 units
Pessimistic volume = 100 units

The expected volume is

$$\frac{100 + 4(450) + 600}{6} = 416.67 = 417 \text{ units}$$

Using all three volume estimates, rather than just the most likely estimates, you explicitly consider the range and direction of uncertainty in judgment. You and your managers might feel (and perhaps survey results indicate) that volume could go as high as 600 or as low as 100. The optimistic volume estimate of 600 units differs from the most likely volume of 450 units by 150 units; the pessimistic volume estimate of 100 units differs by 350 units. Using a beta distribution allows you to take both positive and negative uncertainty into account when predicting expected volume.

Calculate the largest expected volume for each price and compare the revenue and cost resulting from that volume. You can then determine estimated profitability at each price level. Once you have an estimate of expected sales at each price level, unit variable and fixed costs can be subtracted from revenues to obtain the resulting profit contribution. (Remember: Price elasticity of demand refers to revenues, not profits. You must consider the cost as well as revenue implications of demand changes.)

Pricing Under Uncertainty — Decision Trees

When you have to make decisions under uncertainty (which is most of the time), it can help to use a decision model, such as a decision tree or payoff matrix, to make explicit the methods which you implicitly use and to augment these methods with rigorous analysis. A method called Bayesian Prior Analysis can help you to get a better understanding of how you might price under uncertainty.

Suppose that you must make a decision among three prices and that for any of these prices three promotion budgets might be used. Your choice of promotion budget affects sales, so the decision tree depicts all combinations of price and promotion budget. (See Fig. 5.3.) In practice, your market could respond differently to each combination of price and promotion. To keep things simple here, we will assume that one of these possible sales-volume levels will occur in the planning period: 40,000 units, 75,000 units, or 125,000 units.

With the estimated fixed and variable costs for the product or service item, you can project the profit or loss resulting from a particular strategy and market response. A loss of $10,000 will result if you choose a low-price, low-promotion strategy and sales of 150,000 units occurs.

You might want to determine your best price and promotion strategy by choosing the strategy that offers the highest expected profit considering

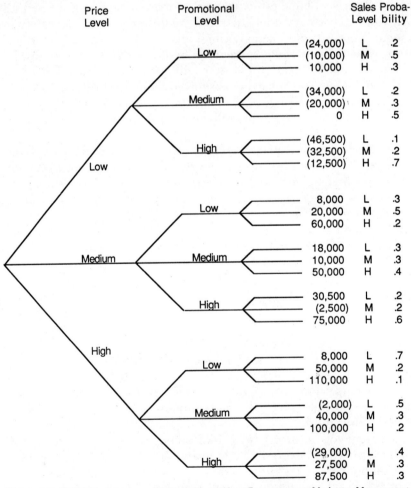

Figure 5.3. Pricing decision tree.   *(Adapted from Alpert* Perspectives in Marketing Management. *Scott, Foresman & Company, Glenview, Ill., 1971, p. 251.)*

all market responses. You could ask your sales managers and sales representatives to give you estimates of the probability of each sales response to each possible price and promotion strategy. Probabilities are assigned to each response, given each strategy combination. The probability of a poor sales response to low price and low promotion might be lower than that for a poor response to high price and low promotion. Normally, higher promotional costs are needed to support a higher price.

Using the estimates supplied by your sales managers and sales representatives, you can then calculate the expected payoff of each strategy by multiplying the payoffs for each sales response by the probabilities that they will occur, given a particular strategy. The expected payoff for the medium-price, high-promotion budget in Figure 5.3 is

$$\text{payoff} = 0.2(-\$30{,}500) + 0.2(-\$2{,}500) + 0.6(\$75{,}000)$$
$$= \$38{,}400$$

With the demand level expected, the best strategy seems to be the one of high price and medium promotional expenditure, with an expected profit payoff of $31,000.

Any strategy involves some risk. There is a 50 percent chance that you will lose $2000 with the high-price, medium-promotion strategy. This loss would be offset by the gains you expect to experience at other times, but if you want to take on less risk you might want to choose the less risky high-price, low-promotion strategy. This option will net at least $8000. On average, though, the highest expected profit strategy will earn more.

A decision tree or payoff matrix analysis can be changed to calculate expected payoffs which reflect different assumptions about the chances of various market responses. This allows you to consider a variety of strategy alternatives and their possible outcomes, to realize the value of having good market information, and to calculate expected profits for each strategy based on estimates of market responses.

Pricing Under Uncertainty — Projecting Expected Profits

As a marketing planner, you will often have to estimate the volume of sales expected at each of several alternative prices, which involves a lot of uncertainty. You are forced to select the most likely volume, even though you cannot estimate the accuracy of a projection. See Fig. 5.4 for a graph of cost-volume-profit relationships.

One solution to the uncertainty problem is to establish a range of prices from which to choose acceptable prices. Use an optimistic, most likely, and

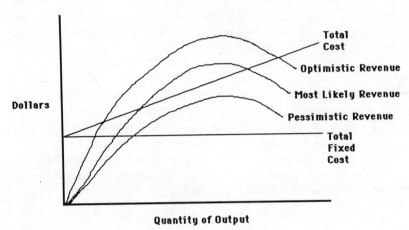

Figure 5.4. Breakeven analysis under uncertainty.

pessimistic volume estimate for each price. Consider the situation shown in Table 5.1.

If we assume a fixed cost of $50,000 to produce the product or service and a variable cost of $3.50 per unit, then total cost and revenue schedules can be created, as shown in Table 5.2.

From such a cost-volume-profit analysis, a lower and upper limit can be evaluated, as well as the break-even point, margin of safety, and operating leverage. You can also evaluate the single expected revenue and profit figure using probability weights that you supply or by using a beta distribution.

After you establish the feasible range in which to select your price, you

Table 5.1. Sales Volume Estimates Based on Several Alternative Prices

Unit price	Pessimistic		Most likely		Optimistic	
	Quantity	Revenue	Quantity	Revenue	Quantity	Revenue
5.00	30,000	150,000	33,000	165,000	38,000	175,000
5.25	28,000	147,000	31,000	162,750	36,000	189,000
5.50	26,000	143,000	29,000	159,500	34,000	187,000
5.75	24,000	138,000	27,000	155,250	32,000	184,000
6.00	22,000	132,000	25,500	150,000	30,000	180,000
6.25	20,000	125,000	23,000	143,750	28,000	175,000
6.50	18,000	117,000	21,000	136,500	26,000	169,000
6.75	16,000	108,000	19,000	128,250	24,000	162,000
7.00	14,000	98,000	18,000	126,000	22,000	154,000

Table 5.2. Total Cost and Revenue Schedule

Unit price	Pessimistic		Most likely		Optimistic	
	Revenue	Total cost	Revenue	Total cost	Revenue	Total cost
5.00	150,000	155,000	165,000	165,500	175,000	168,000
5.25	147,000	148,000	162,750	158,500	189,000	176,000
5.50	143,000	141,000	159,500	151,500	187,000	169,000
5.75	138,000	134,000	155,250	144,500	184,000	162,000
6.00	132,000	127,000	150,000	137,500	180,000	155,000
6.25	125,000	120,000	143,750	130,500	175,000	148,000
6.50	117,000	113,000	136,500	123,500	169,000	141,000
6.75	108,000	106,000	128,250	116,500	162,000	134,000
7.00	98,000	99,000	126,000	113,000	154,000	127,000

Table 5.3. Profit Payoffs Calculated Using Subjective Probability Weights

Unit price	Profit at Quantity Demanded			Expected profit
	Pessimistic ($p = 0.2$)	Most likely ($p = 0.6$)	Optimistic ($p = 0.2$)	
5.00	−5,000	− 500	7,000	100
5.25	−1,000	4,250	13,000	4,950
5.50	2,000	8,000	18,000	8,800
5.75	4,000	10,750	22,000	11,650
6.00	5,000	12,500	25,000	13,500
6.25	5,000	13,250	27,000	14,350
6.50	4,000	13,000	28,000	14,200
6.75	2,000	11,750	28,000	13,050
7.00	−1,000	13,000	27,000	13,000

must calculate the actual expected "payoff" for each price level. Either use a weighted probability payoff scheme, or use the beta distribution. Either method works well, and results depend upon your assumptions about probability weights and/or the range of demand at each price (pessimistic to most likely to optimistic). Using the previous example, subjective probability weights supplied by management or market surveys are used to calculate the profit payoffs shown in Table 5.3 (p represents probability as a fraction of 1.0).*

*See Guiltinan and Paul, Chapter 8; and Bell, Chapter 18.

6

Price Forecasting

Introduction

Price forecasting demands a lot of work — you must know your organization and those of your competitors very well, so you can predict which prices will assure a margin between cost and price that will give an adequate return on investment. Most references on pricing do not address forecasting, and forecasting references often fail to mention price.

Many managers would rather not try to forecast price levels and changes. Instead of predicting prices, some managers may be more interested in obtaining knowledge about matching supply with demand, in gaining technological competitiveness, in analyzing cost trends for substitute products and services, in keeping abreast of government policies affecting pricing freedom, and in forecasting the likely aggressive actions of competitors.

Viewing historic price behavior and using pricing formulas can be less instructive in forecasting prices than a thorough analysis of your markets and your competition. Some companies are able to estimate competitive prices by plotting production experience against cost, extrapolating to get a cost forecast, and then adding a suitable profit margin to arrive at a long-term price forecast.

For many commodities, price follows the pattern of cost. Short-term price deviations which are below a trend during excess capacity and above a trend during times when demand is strong and supply is moderate are common occurrences in capital-intensive industries where operating leverage is critical to profitability. Prices move down with cost, while the overall operating rate is not helped by price decreases.

Price Influences

Many economic factors influence price. A producer of a given product or service might be expected to sell at a price lower than that for the nearest equivalent item, or lower than a government maximum, or lower than foreign competition. The price will probably be higher than total cost at a maximum operating rate (dumping expected). Factors which influence prices include

- U.S. price and demand
- U.S. export prices
- Worldwide price and demand levels
- Availability of substitute products or services
- Raw materials or component parts prices
- Product inventories or service capacities
- Product substitute inventories or service capacities
- Production capacities
- Production costs
- Federal government laws, rules, and regulations
- Other government controls — state, local, and foreign

Cost Influences

Domestic commodity prices are affected by world prices, export prices, substitute product prices, and raw material prices. To forecast prices, you usually should begin with a forecast of costs for minimum and maximum cost producers. You must analyze and project the components of costs along with an appraisal of each competitor's strategy. Some of the major cost producers are

- Labor
- Economies of scale
- Equipment
- Raw materials
- Distribution
- Energy
- Pollution controls
- Construction
- Land
- The experience curve

These costs, especially labor and materials costs, must be forecasted, including those costs for competitive products priced higher and lower than your product or service.

The price forecast derives from forecasts of

- Costs to produce the product or service (high and low cost producers)
- Costs to produce substitutes
- Price elasticity of demand
- Competitive profitabilities
- Competitive strategies
- Capacity additions or shutdowns
- Production or process technology

All aspects of the product, including by-products (if any), must be considered. You must estimate the price elasticity of demand. Is demand inelastic (where raising or lowering prices will not affect demand much) or elastic (changing prices only slightly will result in a great change in demand)? For price-elastic products, large price changes will affect price levels of substitutes (cross-elasticity), and unless a compensation is possible, demand will shift in the long run. How much will demand shift?

You must examine the profitabilities of employing the highest and lowest cost producers at various operating rates (you can use the various PricePlan worksheet programs for this). Armed with this economic information, plus an estimate of your competitors' production capacities, you can begin to guess what competitive strategies are. Competitor capacity expansions or shutdowns may already have been announced. Other contributing factors may have to be estimated.

Through competitive analysis, you might find for a particular product or service and market segment that a low-cost competitor plans to add major capacity well before supply and demand come close to equilibrium levels. The competitor may plan to attack a new market segment with a reduced price to displace rivals with substitutes. Another competitor, a high-cost one, may raise prices and have others follow the lead. All of these strategic competitive moves must be anticipated in price forecasting.

Forecasting prices can require a great deal of work, especially if manual data manipulation methods are used. In addition, economic studies too often miss the mark because of changes in the marketplace, such as revised competitive strategies. Price forecasting can still be valuable, however, if you remember that the precision of a forecast is less important to you than is gaining a good understanding of which factors most affect your strengths and weaknesses as well as those of your rivals.

The Forecasting Process

Forecasting is a highly critical function in businesses and other organizations, serving as the basis for all planning and decision-making activities, especially pricing and sales-volume planning. The organizational planning process usually begins with market and sales forecasts. Business decisions are based implicitly and explicitly on forecasts of the consequences of alternative courses of action.

Forecasting and planning are two different processes. With forecasting, you attempt to describe what will happen for certain decisions and events (assuming no unforeseen changes). When planning, on the other hand, you examine the actions that can be taken which will affect events relating to a given situation. According to Wheelright and Makridakis (1977), the following three elements are common to forecasts:

1. A focus on a specific future time

2. Uncertainty about the future

3. Reliance on historical information

Forecasting seeks to make maximum use of available information to determine the probabilities of future events occurring. A market forecast indicates a probable level of market demand, given an expected level of your industry's marketing effort and your marketing environment. The term *market forecast* refers to a prediction of the demand by a group of buyers for a total industry's products or services. The term *sales forecast* refers to a prediction of the demand for the products and services of one organization only.

Newer and better information is usually available about an industry than about any organization's particular situation. An examination of expected levels of industry marketing effort, market potential, and market demand result in the market forecast. Figure 6.1 illustrates the relationship of demand forecasting to the planning process.

Forecasting Procedures

Wolfe (1966) suggests these basic steps in forecasting:

1. Obtain adequate and accurate benchmark data.

2. Prepare the data properly.

3. Apply more than one forecasting method to the data.

4. Apply sound judgment and intuition.

Benchmark data are time series data relating to sales, product shipments, interest rates, price levels, costs, and so forth. Regression forecasting models rely on such data, but smoothing and qualitative techniques do not (these and other forecasting techniques will be discussed later in this chapter).

Properly preparing data for forecasting is vital for success but is often overlooked by forecasters. Wolfe suggests (and Stacey and Wilson elaborate on) these techniques of data preparation:

1. Leave the data in raw form.

2. Leave the data in raw form but combine several series into one series.

3. Draw graphs to determine relationships between forecast data and either benchmark data or time series data.

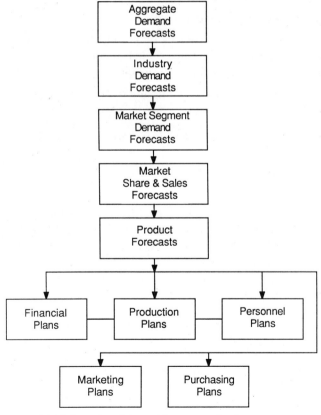

Figure 6.1. Relationship of demand forecasts to the planning process.

4. Develop lead, lag, or coincidental relationships using graphs or statistics.

5. Convert the data to percents or index numbers and develop ratios and first differences in dollars or percents.

6. Separate the data into categories for each known cycle and determine recurrent cycles and cycle states by analogy.

7. Establish critical levels for various series by setting upper and lower historical variation limits.

8. Put the data into statistical form for quantitative analysis.

Wolfe also suggests the following guidelines:

1. Use data that do not fluctuate widely or frequently.

2. Use data at the economy, then industry, then organization levels.

3. Use ratios rather than dollars or units.

4. Eliminate seasonal effects, if possible.

5. Eliminate price level (inflation) influences by converting to constant dollars, then forecasting, then reverting to current dollars. (See also Chapter 11, which discusses the price level problem.)

6. Eliminate population influence by reducing data to a per capita or per organization basis.

Refer to Fig. 6.2 for an overview of demand forecasting techniques.

Forecasting the Economy

The state of the economy heavily influences the demand for goods and services, so forecasting often begins with forecasts of general business conditions. The time period to be forecasted affects the choice of forecasting methods you can use. Long-term forecasts (for two years or more) are based on trend analysis much more than are short-term forecasts.

Long-term forecasts of general business conditions involve trend projections of the Gross National Product (GNP) and its components (personal consumption expenditures, changes in inventories, and others). These projections utilize calculations of historical growth rates, growth-curve fitting, and ratio estimate techniques to relate GNP components to GNP levels. The resulting projections probably are not accurate, but they are sufficient for long-term forecasts.

You usually have the choice of forecasting internally using trend analysis and other methods, adapting other forecasts, or combining approaches.

Many forecasters prefer a combination approach that uses composites of forecasts from internal and external sources.

Econometric Models.   Short-term forecasts of general business conditions are based on highly sophisticated economic and statistical analyses. Major developers of large-scale econometric models include the Wharton School of the University of Pennsylvania, Data Resources, Inc., of Cambridge, Massachusetts, and Chase Econometrics of New York. These models are based on complex systems of simultaneous equations and produce periodic forecasts of the GNP and its components (in current and constant dollars) as well as forecasts of unemployment, capacity utilization, money supply changes, interest rates, and corporate profits. During the rather stable 1960s, these models performed quite well. In the 1970s, the accuracy was often lower due to unforeseen changes such as the Arab oil embargo, but it was still good enough for businesses to rely increasingly on such models for short-term economic forecasts.

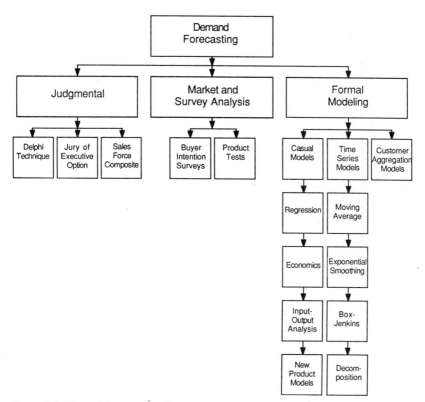

Figure 6.2. Demand forecasting techniques.

Lead-Lag Series. This approach to short-term forecasting of general business conditions is based on cyclical indicators, and it seeks to identify economic time series that lead, coincide with, or lag behind changes in general business activity.

The U.S. Department of Commerce publishes monthly the *Business Conditions Digest,* which contains current values of cyclical economic indicators. Forecasters are most interested in leading indicators, which tend to reach peaks or troughs prior to turns in business activity. Coincident and lagging indicators are used to confirm or reject signals received earlier from leading indicators. See Figs. 6.3 and 6.4 for a list of these indicators.

Leading Indicators

    Average workweek, production workers, manufacturing
    Average weekly initial claims, state unemployment insurance
    Net business formation
    New orders, durable goods industries
    Contracts and orders, plant and equipment
    New building permits, private housing units
    Stock prices, 500 common stocks
    Change in book value, manufacturing and trade inventories
    Industrial materials prices
    Corporate profits after taxes
    Ratio, price to unit labor cost, manufacturing
    Change in consumer installment debt

Roughly Coincident Indicators

    Employees on nonagricultural payrolls
    Unemployment rate, total
    GNP in current dollars
    GNP in constant dollars
    Industrial production
    Personal income
    Manufacturing and trade sales
    Sales of retail stores

Lagging Indicators

    Unemployment rate, persons unemployed 15 weeks and over
    Business expenditures, new plant and equipment
    Book value, manufacturing and trade inventories
    Labor cost per unit of output, manufacturing
    Commercial and industrial loans outstanding, weekly reporting large commercial banks
    Bank rates on short-term business loans

SOURCE: U.S. Department of Commerce, *Business Conditions Digest,* Washington: U.S. Government Printing Office.

Figure 6.3. Cyclical indicators of general business activity.

Formation of Business Enterprises

Net business formation
New business incorporations

New Investment Commitments

New orders, durable goods industries
Construction contracts, total value
Contracts and orders, plant and equipment
New capital appropriations, manufacturing
Manufacturers' new orders, capital goods industries, nondefense
Construction contracts, commercial and industrial
New private housing units started, total
New building permits, private housing units

Inventory Investment and Purchasing

Change in business inventories
Change in book value, manufacturing and trade inventories
Purchased materials, percent of companies reporting higher inventories
Change in book value, manufacturers' inventories of materials and supplies
Buying policy, production materials, percent of companies reporting commitments 60 days or longer
Vendor performance, percent of companies reporting slower deliveries
Change in unfilled orders, durable goods industries

SOURCE: U.S. Department of Commerce, *Business Conditions Digest,* Washington: U.S. Government Printing Office.

Figure 6.4. Cyclical indicators tending to lead industrial business activity.

You may find associations between business activity in your industry and markets and specific leading indicators. Historical orders and shipments for your industry and organization may be compared to leading indicators to find which (if any) of the leading series have tended to reach turning points prior to turns in your industry and organization measures.

Lead-lag forecasting can involve costly and time-consuming data acquisition, maintenance, and handling activities. Computerized database services offered by General Electric Information Services and others provide time-shared access to cyclical indicators and time series from *Business Conditions Digest* and *Survey of Current Business.* Each time series is regularly updated and readily accessible, and the cost is moderate compared to the benefits which can be gained by using them.

Industry and Market Forecasting

Industry and market forecasts are based on relationships between activity measures for an industry and its market and activity measures for the economy. Forecasts are developed for industries rather than markets due to the superiority of the industry data available.

Historical relationships are sought between general or specific business activity measures (the GNP or manufacturers' capital appropriations) and industry orders or shipments. Once these relationships are discovered, economy-level activity measures are forecasted (internally, externally, or both) and industry activity forecasts are derived, based on the assumption that historical relationships will continue. Sometimes, however, historical relationships change as a result of technological change.

Technology Forecasting

Technology forecasting methods evaluate the probability and significance of future technological conditions, using exploratory and normative techniques.

Exploratory Techniques. These techniques are based on trend analysis and rely on quantitative historical data. They include the following:

1. *Curve fitting* uses exponential, power, logistic, and Gompertz curves.

2. *Diffusion process models* measure the rate at which innovations spread through an economy or industry.

3. *Stepwise growth models* study how production capacities change in stair-step fashion for technologies characterized by economies of scale as total industry demand and capacity grow.

4. *Technological progress functions* plot technological capability against cumulative production output to see how the technological process is related to the experience curve.

5. *Substitution models* seek to measure the rate at which new technologies are substituted for old ones. (They are relatable to diffusion models.)

Normative Techniques. Normative techniques are based on assessment of the future by experts, are largely qualitative in nature, and are relatively free of historical influence. These are particularly useful for very long-range forecasts and where technological discontinuities are likely to occur. For example, new product components may profoundly affect product performance, such as new computer processor chips, which significantly improve the performance of existing machines.

1. *The Delphi Method* pools opinions of a group of experts, its users assuming group opinion to be more accurate than any one expert's.

2. *Cross-impact analysis* is an extension of the Delphi Method that seeks to examine interrelationships between forecasted events and items. A matrix of cross-effects of events is established along with linkages among events, strengths of relationships, and the nature of relationships.

Selecting an Appropriate Industry Forecasting Technique

Your planning situation will be unique but can be viewed as similar to that of other product or service offerings. The following sections highlight typical criteria used to choose from among the various forecasting techniques available.

Characteristics of the Situation. Wheelright and Makridakis suggest the following six major characteristics to consider in selecting appropriate forecasting techniques:

1. *Time horizon*

   - immediate-term (less than one month)
   - short-term (1 to 3 months)
   - medium-term (3 months to 2 years)
   - long-term (over 2 years)

2. *Level of detail*—general industry level to specific products or services
3. *Number of items*—hundreds of products or services to just a few
4. *Control versus planning requirements*—very responsive forecasts for control, very complex ones for planning
5. *Stability*—the degree of historical change in data
6. *Existing planning procedures*—initial choices influenced by existing procedures, evolution to upgraded techniques

Type of Product or Service. All products and services can be classified into one of three groups:

1. Products or services used directly in the production process (such as major and accessory equipment)
2. Products or services incorporated directly into the products or services of the producer (such as component parts and materials)
3. Products or services consumed in the process of production (such as operating supplies and services)

These product types are very different from each other, so each will require a different forecasting approach.

Characteristics of the Technique. Data analysis methods vary in their purpose and usefulness when applied to your specific data and planning situation. Carefully review your situation in light of these characteristics of forecasting techniques (identified by Wheelright and Makridakis):

1. *Time horizon*—quantitative techniques for longer terms

2. *Data patterns*—seasonal, cyclical, and trend patterns

3. *Model type*—time vs. other data variation determinants used as variables.

4. *Cost*

5. *Accuracy*

6. *Ease of application*

Also, you need to consider the data required for the technique to be useful versus the data available to you at the time required to develop the forecast.

Organization-Level Forecasting

The basic procedure in organization-level forecasting is to forecast sales or costs as a percentage or ratio of the preceding forecast. Industry forecasts serve as the basis for organization forecasts with market share as the link between forecasts.

Nonconditional forecasts of organization market share for your organization's markets and market segments can be prepared, assuming there is no change in the level of your industry's marketing efforts or your marketing environment. Such forecasts would determine the portion of market share that would remain constant.

Conditional forecasts of organization market share are prepared next, based on expected changes in your industry and organization marketing effort levels, along with expected changes in the marketing environment. These forecasts require you to specify market and organization demand functions for the products or services in question.

Product or Service-Level Forecasting

A product- or service-demand forecast is made as a percentage or ratio of previous forecasts. Product- or service-demand forecasts are often implicitly combined with organization forecasts to determine an organization's share of a given product or service demand at the industry level.

You might forecast the demand for your organization's product or service directly as a market share of the demand industrywide for such an item—look at the total product demand and then at your fraction of the market. Or you might forecast your organization's market share of total industry demand for the product or service and then forecast the demand for your organization's product or service as a percentage or ratio of your total organization forecast—look at your fraction of the demand for the product and then adjust from your forecasts for all of your products. The first approach avoids the possibility of erroneously allocating an organization forecast across a product or service line. As with organization forecasts, you need to prepare both nonconditional and conditional product- or service-demand forecasts, based on analysis of your market and organization demand functions for the product or service item.

Subjective Forecasting Methods

You can choose from a variety of forecasting methods ranging from hunches to complex mathematical equations. The simplest, and often the fastest, methods are those which require largely subjective judgment. There are many such methods, three of which are discussed here.

Internal Organization Data

Sales Force Composite Estimates. This method is based on examining internal organization data generated by a sales force, with each sales representative asked to estimate sales in his or her particular territory. These individual estimates are combined and reviewed at successively higher levels of management so that the opinions of managers at each level are incorporated into the overall forecast.

These forecasts have several advantages. One is that they can be easily divided by territory, branch, sales representative, or product or service. Sales representatives are closest to customers and may have better knowledge and insight into market conditions than anyone else. This is particularly important for new products or services or ones for which market conditions are changing rapidly. This method may provide higher motivation for sales personnel because of the greater involvement it gives them in the planning process.

Several disadvantages must also be noted. Because this is a subjective method, results may be affected by individual biases. Sales representatives may be too heavily influenced by recent market successes or setbacks, or they may be habitually pessimistic or optimistic in their estimates. Also, sales representatives may be unaware of important economic developments or marketing plans that may influence sales in the territory. They may not have the time or motivation to prepare careful estimates.

Jury of Executive Opinion. This common approach is based on the examination of internal organization data generated by a group of key executives and involves averaging individual estimates or holding group discussions that result in a single estimate. A senior officer might review estimates from sales, production, and finance executives and then apply his or her individual judgment to arrive at the final estimate.

One advantage of this method is that it can give you a forecast in a fairly short time. It focuses a variety of views on the subject and can build team support. Disadvantages include:

- The high cost of executive time
- The difficulty of breaking down estimates by geographic area and product or service
- Biases deriving from individual attitudes and situations
- The difficulty of weighing individual estimates

External Organization Data

User or Buyer Intentions and Expectations.   You can seek subjective opinions from people outside your organization. The user-buyer intention or expectation method requires that customers or potential customers be polled about purchasing plans for the future. You might use mail questionnaires, telephone surveys, or personal surveys.

A probability sample of users or buyers is developed and each respondent is asked how much he or she would buy of a given product or service under stated conditions. Respondents are then asked what proportion of total purchases would be from your organization and perhaps what factors would influence the choice of supplier.

An advantage of this method is that you get an opportunity to learn some of the reasons behind user or buyer intentions and expectations. You might get new views of your product or service strengths and weaknesses as well as other reasons why customers will or will not buy the item from you. You can thus use this method to plan new product or service developments or to improve established items.

The user-buyer intentions and expectations method has the following disadvantages.

- It may require a large staff and considerable time.
- It may annoy important customers.
- Stated intentions may not translate into actual buying or usage behavior.
- Nonresponses from key buyers or users can represent significant error.

Several sampling services regularly produce reports on consumer buying intentions for such items as new housing, furniture, appliances, and automobiles. These services ask consumers whether they intend to buy items during a stated time period.

Industrial buyer intention surveys may involve questions about equipment and materials and can be conducted by independent services or by surveys of your own customers and potential customers.

Market Tests. A direct test of the market for your product or service is needed when you want to forecast sales of a new item or sales of an existing item through new distribution channels or to new markets or market segments. Buyer opinions depend on buyers knowing product or service prices, availability, reliability, and amount and type of support available from your organization. If buyers or users do not plan purchases carefully or are inconsistent in their buying or usage, you may not be able to depend on their responses to an opinion survey. The direct market test is desirable then, because you can save time and expense by getting information about actual buying or usage. A disadvantage of the market test is that it can require a large staff of experts and can be very expensive initially. In addition, accurate testing may be difficult to set up and execute.

Objective Forecasting Methods

Personal judgment may be biased, so statistical calculations may be desirable. Patterns in sales and costs and relationships among sales and other variables can often be observed, measured, and incorporated into forecasts. Like subjective methods, statistical methods can also have disadvantages.

Time Series Methods

Simple Cumulative Averages. You can use averages to project demand or cost data. One way you can average time series data is to add all observations for past periods and divide by the number of periods. This is simple but useful only if you are forecasting the average of a series that has a consistent horizontal trend. An average will not respond rapidly to any random fluctuations or material change in the data over time.

If you sold a product or service for 24 months and the average demand was stable at 1000 units per month for the first 12 months and then at 1500 units per month for the most recent 12 months, the demand in the latter periods will have stabilized at an average level of 1250 units per month. You can see that this method underestimates demand for the most recent months. This will always be true of this method as long as the first 12 months are included in the average. If you experience a continuous rising trend, the average will never be accurate, and you should not use this method.

Simple Moving Averages. Unlike simple cumulative averages, simple moving averages keep a running account of a predetermined number of observations. Each period a new observation is included in the average, while the oldest observation is discarded. Simple moving averages give all observations equal weight, so if too many periods are included in a moving average, the average will not respond rapidly to random fluctuations or material change, as with cumulative averages.

If the moving average does not move rapidly with the data, the forecast is called *stable*. It is desirable when you need to avoid being fooled by random fluctuations but less desirable when a strong trend is present.

A forecast is called *responsive* if it adapts quickly to true changes in the base level of the data. This is desirable when a strong trend is present, but if a forecast is immediately responsive to changes in the data, it is susceptible to rapid fluctuations, which may be random occurrences. In practice, it is difficult to achieve the best features of stability and responsiveness in the same forecast. The more periods you include in a moving average, the more stable is the forecast, but the responsiveness is slow.

Weighted Moving Averages. While simple moving average assigns equal weights to all observations in a forecast, a weighted moving average assigns more weight to some values than to others. The objective of weighting is to allow recent data to influence the forecast more than older data. If there is a long-run trend, a weighted average with more emphasis on recent data is desired, but the forecast will still lag behind the actual data.

The moving average weighs the past N observations with the value $1/N$, with N remaining constant. The larger N is, the greater the smoothing effect on the forecasted data. Usually, you use moving averages to forecast only one period in advance. This can be expressed as follows:

$$S_{t+1} = \frac{1}{N} \sum_{i=t-N+1}^{t} X_i \frac{X_t - X_{t-N}}{N} + S_t$$

where

$$S_t = \text{forecast for time period } t$$
$$X_t = \text{observed value in time period } t$$
$$N = \text{number of values included in average}$$

In this equation S_{t+1} is a function of the preceding moving-average forecast S_t. The larger the value of N, the smaller the value of $(X_t - X_{t-N})/N$ and the greater the smoothing effect.

Exponential Smoothing. An extension of the weighted moving average, the exponentially smoothed average keeps a running average which is adjusted each period in proportion to the difference between the latest actual observation and the latest value of the average. The following equation shows an exponentially smoothed average:

$$SF_t = aA_{t-1} + (1 - a)SF_{t-1}$$

$$\text{or} \quad SF_{t-1} + a(A_{t-1} - SF_{t-1})$$

where

SF_t = smoothed forecast for time period t
SF_{t-1} = smoothed forecast for time period $t - 1$
a = smoothing constant for weight of previous time periods ($0 < = a < = 1$)
A_{t-1} = actual observation in time period $t - 1$

The smoothing constant a is a number between 0 and 1 and can be set to a value that will make the equation fit past data better than other values of a. It thus influences the stability and responsiveness of the forecast. If a is set equal to 0, an old forecast would not be adjusted for a more accurate fit, regardless of the actual observations. This means that the resulting forecast is stable, but it would not respond to any changes in the actual observations.

If a is set equal to 1, the latest forecast would equal the last observation, so the forecast would be very responsive but not stable. You will want to choose a value between 0 and 1, perhaps between 0.1 and 0.3. The initial forecast must be generated by a method other than exponential smoothing to begin a series of exponentially smoothed forecast values.

Adaptive Filtering. This technique is based on an iterative process that determines weights that minimize forecasting error by minimizing the average mean-squared forecasting error, which can be expressed as follows:

$$W' = W + 2ke\mathbf{X}$$

where

W' = revised set of weights
W = old set of weights
k = learning constant
e = forecasting error in the last period
$\mathbf{X}$ = vector of observed values

The revised weights should equal the old set of weights adjusted for the most recently observed error. $1/N$ will work for an initial set of weights, where N might correspond to the length of a complete cycle in the data pattern. Choosing the learning constant can be a difficult decision, and the procedures to revise weights usually require computer support.

The Box-Jenkins Method.   This method is the most general of the short-term forecasting techniques and is one of the most powerful tools available. Using the Box-Jenkins method, you can develop an adequate forecast from almost any data, but the method's complexity requires considerable user expertise. Within the Box-Jenkins philosophy are the following three general classes of models for describing any type of stationary process:

- An autoregressive model (AR)
- A moving average model (MA)
- An autoregressive moving average model (ARMA)

Decomposition Methods.   In many cases, the time series pattern can be separated into other patterns that identify each component of the series separately. This breakdown can often improve forecasting accuracy. For instance, retail price levels often show patterns of a permanent upward trend over time, with a temporary upward swing at Christmas and temporary downward swing at other times of the year. This means that a forecast could be decomposed into a seasonal cycle superimposed upon an upward trend line.

The decompositional methods assume that all series consist of patterns plus random errors. The purpose of using such methods is to decompose the overall pattern into trend, cycle, and seasonal elements. This can be expressed as follows:

$$X_t = f(I_t, T_t, C_t, E_t)$$

where

X_t = position of time series at time t
I_t = seasonal component at time t
T_t = trend component at time t
C_t = cyclical component at time t
E_t = random error component at time t

Often a multiplicative form of the function is used:

$$X_t = I_t \times T_t \times C_t \times E_t$$

Or an additive form may be used:

$$X_t = I_t + T_t + C_t + E_t$$

The most widely used decompositional method is the Census II method developed at the U.S. Bureau of the Census. The X-11 form of this method considers trading days, smoothing for extreme points, varying-length moving averages for random components with different average levels, and so forth. This method does not have a sound statistical base but rather is intuitive and geared to the practitioner, in contrast to the complex Box-Jenkins method. The Census II method seems to be appropriate for short-term or medium-term forecasts, so it is used for the study of macroeconomic series.

Causal Methods

An alternative to the time-series methods is to express demand as a function of a certain number of factors, such as buyer income, age, sex, education level, and other buyer characteristics, that determine actual sales demand. These forecasts are useful for long-term estimating because they are not strictly time-dependent.

Regression Models.   Regression models often specify the structure between the observed data and underlying causes of the data's pattern. For example, if you use the number of employees as a potential estimator of sales potential, you might use the following form:

$$\text{Sales} = a_0 + a_1 \text{ (number of employees)} + \text{random error}$$

or, more generally,

$$Y_t = a + bx$$

where

$$b = \frac{n\sum_{i=1}^{n} X_i Y_i - \sum_{i=1}^{n} X_i \sum_{i=1}^{n} Y_i}{n\sum_{i=1}^{n} X_i^2 - \left[\sum_{i=1}^{n} X_i\right]^2}$$

and

$$a = \bar{Y} - b\bar{X} = \frac{\sum_{i=1}^{n} Y_i}{n} - b\frac{\sum_{i=1}^{n} X_i}{n} = \frac{\sum_{i=1}^{n} Y_i - b\sum_{i=1}^{n} X_i}{n}$$

where

$\bar{Y}$ = arithmetic mean of the dependent variable
$\bar{X}$ = arithmetic mean of the independent variable
n = number of data points or X, Y pairs
$\sum$ = a summation of all values to the right
Y = actual values of the dependent variable
X = values of the independent variable

Linear regression will give you the values for a_0 and a_1, which you can plug into the above equation and solve for the sales figure. You plug in different amounts for the variable you use for the predictor (the number of employees in the example above) and create a set of points which can be plotted on a graph as a straight line.

Instead of using time as the variable to explain demand, as with time series methods, you may want to use an economic indicator. You would most like to find an indicator that moves before your sales or costs (a leading indicator) and that is stable enough to use for prediction. Simple linear regression will fit a line to a series of points that indicate past values of one dependent variable (sales or costs) and one independent variable (the predictor, perhaps an economic indicator). You fit the line to the data points so that the sum of all the squared deviations from the points to the line will be minimized.

It is likely that the proper use of variables in addition to an economic indicator, such as promotional expenditure or the price of the good or service, will better explain sales or costs. Multiple regression establishes a mathematical relationship between a dependent variable and two or more independent variables.

The *coefficient of linear correlation* tells how closely a group of points coincides with a straight line and can be expressed as follows:

$$r = \frac{n\sum X_i Y_i - \sum_{i=1}^{n} X_i \sum_{i=1}^{n} Y_i}{\left\{\left[n\sum_{i=1}^{n} X_i^2 - \sum_{i=1}^{n} X_i^2 \right]\left[n\sum_{i=1}^{n} Y_i^2 - \sum_{i=1}^{n} Y_i^2 \right]\right\}^{1/2}}$$

The coefficient can be positive or negative. A positive r indicates that large values of X are associated with large values of Y. As X increases, Y also increases. A negative r says that Y declines as X increases. The closer the absolute value of r is to 1.0, the better the line fits the points.

The standard error of the estimate, s_y, is based on the mean square vertical deviation of the points from the trend line, rather than the mean, as with the standard deviation. This can be expressed as follows:

$$s_y = \left| \frac{\sum(Y - Y_t)^2}{n - 2} \right|^{1/2} \quad \text{or} \quad \left| \frac{\sum Y^2 - a\sum(XY)}{n - 2} \right|$$

You should compare the standard errors of your forecasts to see which model fits the data best. There should be some logical relationship or explanation for the variables you use in any regression models. A strong relationship is useful only if it actually predicts through a known relationship among the variables.

Econometric Models. Econometric models can be used for predicting economic variables of a geographic region, sales in an entire industry, or sales of an individual organization. These models often use several regression equations at one time. The equations represent the forces that variables exert on your observed data.

You can use a model for prediction if values of the variables are substituted into the equations in a fashion similar to that used with regression models. As with regression, residual errors (unexplained variations about the predicted values) still occur, and you would usually prefer a model that minimizes the unexplained variation.

Monitoring and Controlling Forecasts

Sales or cost patterns are seldom static, and forecasts should strive to move with the data or even anticipate movements. You will almost always be gaining and losing customers or clients, and the level of activity with existing ones will vary. Therefore, you should always try to periodically review and revise your forecasts, perhaps even changing the estimation method you use.

You could use a *tracking signal,* which is the ratio of the running sum of forecast errors to the mean absolute deviation. The tracking signal equation is expressed as follows:

$$\text{Tracking signal} = \frac{\sum_{t=1}^{n}(A_t - F_t)}{(A_t - F_t)/n}$$

where

$$A_t = \text{actual value for period } t$$
$$F_t = \text{forecast value for period } t$$

The tracking signal is recalculated each time actual data for a period become available and each time the forecast is updated. The tracking signal should remain fairly small. If observed data depart significantly from your forecast for several periods, the running sum of forecast errors (the numerator in the preceding equation) will grow, causing the tracking signal to become too large. When the tracking signal moves outside of some predetermined range, it trips a signal, indicating that you should reevaluate the data pattern and the forecasting method used.

When you are using a computer for forecasting, the computer may be programmed to print only the expected values unless the tracking signal limit is exceeded, at which time an exception report can be printed to display the past history, which will enable you to diagnose the cause of the deviation. If you use exponential smoothing, the forecasting system can be programmed to change the value of the smoothing constant so the forecast will be more responsive. Adaptive smoothing performs this change.

Summary of Objective Forecasting Methods

Forecasting is important in pricing analysis and control as well as in other functions within your organization. You must make long-range, medium-range, and short-range decisions, and all these require that you make some assumptions about the future. Forecasting is important to your decision making because the projections generated indicate when decisions are needed, determine which of your alternatives are feasible, and help you to determine which alternative solution you should select.

Forecasts of demand and costs are important because you can't always control demand or costs, but you must provide goods or services in response to them. Sales forecasts, for instance, are basic inputs to your financial plans, personnel plans, facilities plans, and marketing plans. You may use short- to medium-range forecasts to plan production, to procure inputs to production, and to schedule the transformation of production inputs into goods or services. Specific forecasts might be updated each week or month. Long-range forecasts may be made quarterly or annually to aid you in making long-range plans for facilities, research and development programs, and marketing strategies.

You might wish to use several types of forecasting methods to estimate the future. Subjective or statistical methods can be used. You might get your source data from inside or outside your organization. Data internal to your organization can be used for forecasting by simple moving averages, weighted moving averages, exponential smoothing, or time series analysis. Data external to your organization can be used with one of the above methods or with index correlation and econometric forecasting.

You can use moving average and exponential smoothing methods for short-term forecasts, which do not require extensive historical data. Time series analysis and higher-order exponential smoothing are useful when knowing about seasonal variations is important to your planning. You will need considerable amounts of historical data to provide estimates of the consistency of any seasonal indexes.

Regression analysis can be useful to determine trends in time series analysis, which can be extended for estimates of long-range changes. Regression analysis can also help you to estimate the relationship between sales or costs and some index of economic activity. Extrapolating any pattern from data is always subject to turning points in the pattern, and you should compare the forecast made by one method with other forecasts and compare any forecast to what common sense suggests to you before you base your plans on such a forecast.

7

Pricing Considerations for Service Organizations

Differences Between Goods and Services

Marketing services is different from marketing goods. The basic marketing principles used to market goods are applicable to service marketing. However, there are several service marketing attributes which are very different, some of which have a direct impact on service prices. Many of these attributes have both advantages and disadvantages. In the following sections we will examine some of the key differences between goods and services and how service pricing is affected.

Intangibility of Services

Products are tangible — they can be seen and touched. Services are intangible, which is the one characteristic which most differentiates services from physical products. Intangibility is usually seen as a disadvantage for services, but it can create advantages. For example, goods are easily recognizable and definable, so customers can make selections based on their perceptions of tangible items, whereas customer curiosity about intangible services may lead to sales.

Some goods, such as many foods, are perishable. A service is not immediately perishable (it won't physically spoil), even though it may lose its value to a buyer. Also, physical products must be stored, which usually involves an inventory carrying cost, which may include costs to maintain the goods, costs to move products, and interest costs of financing cash-flow shortages. Raw materials, component parts, work in process, and finished goods must all be stored. Services do not incur inventory carrying costs.

Tangibility allows goods marketers to use creative product design, packaging, and advertising. Services are more difficult to promote because you must stimulate people's senses of sight, sound, touch, and smell, but the often high costs of appealing promotions can be avoided, too.

One other advantage of physical products is that they can often be produced at one time and sold at another. Services, too, can be presold but can't be presented to customers in stores in the same way that furniture, appliances, automobiles, and a host of other consumer products can be. Also, goods are usually returnable for a refund but services are not. Sometimes it is difficult to even decide when a service has been completed, as with development of custom-designed computer software whose specifications change while the service is being rendered.

Sometimes institutions which offer intangible services emphasize tangible items in their marketing. For example, bank financial services are marketed with tangibility in mind: Fancy printed checks are available, bank facilities are attractive and comfortable, and premiums in the form of physical products are given as incentives to customers. Insurance companies have a tangibility problem, because insurance policies are intangible but often expensive and difficult to justify. As a result, insurance companies are turning to company positioning strategies, where the company image is promoted to potential buyers instead of just product attributes.

Government Intervention

Services are intangible and difficult to judge accurately, which seems to cause governments to want to control the marketing of services. Services cannot be returned if the buyer is dissatisfied, it is often not possible to sample a service before buying, and a service cannot be repossessed, so some consumer protection is desirable.

One form of government intervention is licensing, as is done with mechanics, bartenders, beauticians, and barbers. Another form is accreditation, as with the medical, dental, legal, and accounting professions. Formal accreditation may require many years of formal training at approved institutions and a certain number of years of experience. Accreditation may be accompanied by rigorous examination.

The federal and state governments directly regulate some services, such as banking, insurance, and freight hauling. Banks and savings and loan institutions must be chartered at the federal and/or state level, investment firms at the federal level, and insurance companies at the state level.

Proximity to Buyers

Most services must be performed close to buyers, because location is used by the buyer as a basis for selecting the service product, either out of convenience or necessity. Retail outlets must be located near potential customers, and the same is true for service organizations. A manufacturer, on the other hand, need not be located near the end user. Indeed, some manufacturers are able to sell their goods around the world.

The delivery of a service is often personal. The cost of transporting a service product to the customer must be factored into prices, or the customer will have to travel to the service provider. If transportation costs are not included in prices, a seller can in effect be subsidizing purchasers. If the transportation cost becomes too great, prices will have to rise and buyers may look elsewhere for the service.

Distribution methods, including telemarketing, electronic funds transfer, and information transfer, are sometimes used to offset the proximity problem, but often these methods meet with little success because buyers still want personal services delivered to them. Financial markets are not as much of a problem for small sellers as they once were, because small institutions can now extend credit by tapping into larger national and international financial markets and thus compete effectively against large institutions who attempt to use remote marketing methods.

Distribution

Services are distributed differently than goods. Customers must come to the service establishment or the service provider must go to the customer, and at least some part of the distribution is always person-to-person. This limits the geographic range for marketing services. There is a limit to the pick-up and delivery services that can be offered. Attempts to market some services at a distance from buyers will not succeed if customers want to develop a feeling of trust through personal contact. For services which are expensive, people prefer to have personal contact with their supplier.

Sometimes a service supplier can combine services with other goods or services available to users at the same time. Sears now offers insurance and real estate brokerage services in retail stores where customers already shop. This may enable Sears to branch into other financial services with much less difficulty than many other companies might have.

Price Effects of Differences between
Goods and Services

Differences between goods and services often translate into differences in prices. Service providers can often charge higher prices if a service can be made to appear more tangible. An accredited educational institution which offers a diploma (a tangible product) and a good job-placement record can charge more than one which does not. If a service is guaranteed in writing (a tangible evidence of value), that service is worth more to a customer.

The costs of licensing, examinations, professional credentials, and government regulation cause an increase in service prices. As the airline, trucking, banking, brokerage, and telecommunications industries become deregulated, prices are falling. The resulting increase in competition means that service providers will have to become more sophisticated in all aspects of their marketing programs, not just in their pricing.

Lack of proximity can increase service prices. This occurs as the result of transportation costs or the cost of locating facilities near customers. The higher costs of getting close to the customer are translated into higher prices. Some distribution methods also raise prices. Highly valuable personnel are more costly to hire and are more costly to train and transport to the customer.

The various characteristics of service products tend to increase their prices relative to physical products. If service providers can manipulate service characteristics proficiently, profitability will be kept high. Service-product characteristics must be considered in detail and factored into the overall marketing of services. The failure to understand differences among goods and service can result in faulty price planning and implementation.

Service Pricing in Practice

Service organizations, like goods-oriented ones, need to provide for the costs of adequate salaries, staff training and continuing education, office administration, and downtime. In addition to nonbillable time, a service organization might analyze billable time to determine sources of revenue.

Service organizations need to earn a profit (or budget surplus) in order to supply working capital for continuing operations and organizational growth. There is at the same time increasing societal pressure to minimize service fees. Continued (and possibly increasing) government intervention in service organization operations will restrict managers' abilities to price their services as they see fit.

Profit (Surplus) Maximization

The idea of profit maximization need not be foreign to service organizations. By ensuring present and future financial strength, service organizations are better able to serve their customers. Profit maximization means simply that an organization must set prices above costs so that purchase of services will supply enough revenue to cover costs and ensure a surplus for organizational development.

In a totally free market environment, there is little price elasticity — demand will fall as prices are increased. Services previously considered as needed are redefined as optional, and customers seek other service suppliers, attempt to provide the services themselves, or simply do not seek service assistance. The key to profit maximization is to set service fees high enough above operation costs to earn the maximum revenue per service offered, yet low enough so that there will be adequate continued demand.

As prices increase from zero, profitability will improve to the point where market resistance becomes significant. Further price increases will result in lower demand for services as customers seek alternatives. The drop in services purchased, with the fixed costs operating a service organization still incurs, may result in much lower profit levels. Maximum profitability is attained when there is sustained demand for services (usually at intermediate price levels).

Fees should not be set so low that they cause customers to underrate the quality of the services offered. Individuals and organizations are not equal in ability or performance, so they should not expect the same returns. In professional firms, for instance, senior professionals charge higher fees than other members of the firm, but they produce higher total profitability only when there is adequate demand at these higher fee rates.

Objective Price Setting

Objective price setting means setting a fixed fee for a service (or an hourly charge-out rate) and multiplying that fee by the number of services used (or hours worked). Attorneys and management consultants, for example, often use a standard hourly rate for each type of service or for each employee, based on experience level. Only accurate items (number of services or hours plus disbursements) are used. These fees can be adjusted before customers are billed, if necessary.

The objective price-setting approach has the advantage of being consistent and easy to implement. The disadvantage is that it usually fails to account for individual customer perceptions of service value. Also, fixed fees probably will not be negotiated with customers, with the result that fees may be too low or too high relative to those of rival service providers.

Subjective Price Setting

Subjective price setting involves adjustment of the objectively determined price for perceived value and acceptability to the customer. If time and service records are not kept, the actual billing may be only an estimate. Subjective elements of service fees include

- Estimates of service production efficiency
- Comparative skill and experience of service provider
- Reputation of service provider
- Type and difficulty of work
- Inconvenience to customer
- Unusual expenses
- Market price levels
- Overtime (if required)
- Service value and acceptability to customer

Many services might be systematic to produce, so objective billing is often appropriate. On the other hand, production of many other services closely resembles an art, so a subjective billing approach often more truly expresses the value of services.

Whichever approach you choose for service price setting, consider these possible legitimate complaints about high fee rates:

- Inexperience of the service provider
- False starts in service production
- Lack of adequate supervision
- Use of overqualified senior personnel
- Performance of unnecessary service work

Cost-Oriented Service Pricing

Many firms base their prices on the costs of providing services. The major advantage of cost-oriented price setting is its simplicity over demand-oriented price setting (see Table 7.1). Cost-oriented prices appear fairer — the service provider will retain an adequate profit level, and the customer is not subject to unusually high prices when demand is high. Many service firms use a cost orientation in their fee setting.

The margin and total cost might be equated to the value of the firm if

Table 7.1. Cost-Oriented Service Pricing

Top Management Salaries	$ 38,000	31.4%
Staff Salaries (A)	12,100	
Staff Salaries (B)	16,000	
Staff Salaries (C)	10,200	
Total Staff Salaries	38,300	31.7%
Other Fixed Costs	36,700	30.3%
Required Return on Investment	8,000	6.6%
Total Cost	$121,000	100.0%
Margin	35,000	35.0%
Total Revenue Required	$156,000	

stock is traded in the open market, where valuation is based on pure return on investment calculations.

Once an organization has determined its costs and the prices required to maintain adequate profit levels, it can work backward, using the weighted value of each employee to determine the appropriate hourly fee for each individual. Different service supplier employees have different value to customers, and by determining the relative worth of each individual it is possible to calculate hourly charge-out rates necessary to achieve the required revenue, as demonstrated in Tables 7.2 and 7.3:

Demand-Oriented Pricing

Many service organizations use demand-oriented pricing, charging what the market will allow, with little regard for the costs of providing services. The resulting prices need not be high (as when there is high demand).

Table 7.2. Annual Billable Hours

	Days	Total hours
Total	365	2737.5
Less: Weekends	104	780.0
Holidays	10	75.0
Vacations	14	105.0
Personal days	5	37.5
Administration	30	225.0
Waiting times	7	52.5
Extra lunch time	8	60.0
Extra break time	7	52.5
Training	12	90.0
Total nonbillable time	197	1477.5
Total billable time	168	1260.0

Table 7.3. Service Fee Determination

Employee position	Value weight	Billable hours	Weighted hours	Weighted fee	Fees earned	Charge rate
A	8	1200	9600	7.50	$ 72,000	60.00
B	6	600	3600	7.50	27,000	45.00
C	2	970	1940	7.50	14,550	15.00
D	5	1040	5200	7.50	39,000	37.50
Totals		3810	20,340		$152,550	

Rising competition and faltering demand may result in lower charge-out fees. It is often useful to try to charge different prices to different customers in order to maximize revenue. This, in general, is referred to as *price discrimination.*

Customer discrimination may occur where prices vary with customer ability to pay. *Service discrimination* exists where fees for services vary with the type of service. *Time discrimination* may occur where different rates are charged based on demand, discounts for early work, and overtime rates. *Location discrimination* occurs when different rates are charged in different geographic locations. All of these types of price discrimination require market segmentation to determine marketing costs, demand, and profitability of each market segment.

Competition-Oriented Pricing

Under this method, prices are set relative to prices charged by competitive service providers in the same or similar markets. This method allows simplicity in price setting — just find out what rivals are charging and price accordingly. The disadvantage is that this does not always allow precise pricing of unique or specialized services to unique or specialized market segments. Segmentation information about rival organizations is sometimes very difficult to obtain.

Recommendations for Service Price-Setting

Webb (1982) lists the following major considerations in determining price structures for service organization profit:

1. Base prices on cost to some degree.
2. Use selective price increases where competition prevents general price increases.

3. Cover direct costs, fixed expenses, and a reasonable profit margin.
4. Review prices continuously.
5. Use break-even analysis to examine effects of fixed-cost changes, direct-expense changes, and volume changes, and the resulting profits.

Break-even price-setting requires gathering data to determine minimum revenue to cover variable expenses and fixed expenses and to guarantee a reasonable margin of profit. Determining the break-even point requires a clear segregation of direct (variable) costs from fixed costs. Use break-even analysis to examine relationships among costs, volume, and profits in order to support your choices for setting and changing prices. This will ensure that you are not making blind decisions.*

---

*The major source for this section is Webb, Chapter 12.

8

Cost-Volume-Profit (Break-Even) Analysis

When you make key pricing decisions, you should always consider the minimum sales revenue needed to cover your costs. Revenue results from selling a certain number of units of a product or service at a certain average price per unit (revenue = quantity × price). The quantity factor is crucial because it represents the number of units that must be sold to recover costs (and to earn a profit, if possible). Cost-volume-profit (CVP) analysis is a valuable and powerful tool for controlling the relationship between your marketing mix and the results you get for your expenditures.

CVP analysis, often referred to as break-even analysis, allows you to evaluate how revenue, fixed costs, and variable costs affect levels of profit. The analysis identifies the break-even point, where total revenue equals total cost (profit equals zero).

To get the most out of CVP analysis, your system of cost accounting must be able to separate each relevant cost category into its fixed and variable components. On a total cost level, fixed or variable refers to whether or not the cost amount varies with the number of units of output.

Fixed-Period Costs

For our purposes, a fixed-cost item amount is assumed to remain constant during a specified time period, even when no units of output are produced and sold. (See Figure 8.1.) Some examples of fixed-period costs are

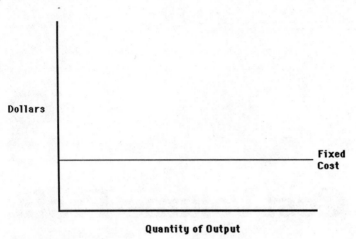

Figure 8.1. Fixed cost chart.

- R & D or design expenses
- Building, equipment, machinery, fixtures, and other capital expenditures
- Administrative and management expenses
- Insurance, interest, property taxes, leases, and depreciation expenses

Advertising expenses are usually considered a fixed-cost item, although advertising commitments can be canceled. Depreciation of assets or investments is usually fixed because the actual asset usage during a time period is irrelevant for most depreciation schemes. Of course, machinery, equipment, and buildings can be sold or depreciated at rates reflecting actual asset usage.

Direct Costs per Unit (Variable Costs)

Direct costs per unit are those costs that can be directly attributed to the product or service and vary with the number of units sold, such as

- Raw materials, supplies, or component parts
- Labor and supervision
- Production costs
- Variable administrative expenses

- Packaging, handling, and shipping costs
- Commissions and bonuses to wholesalers, retailers, agents, and brokers
- Unit royalty or license fees
- Bad debts
- Returns and refurbishing costs

Direct materials and direct labor costs can be determined on a per unit basis, as can direct machine costs (when used). Unlike fixed costs, these costs are not incurred when there is no production output. In marketing, commissions are a direct (or variable) cost. See Fig. 8.2 for an illustration of variable costs.

Contribution Margin

The contribution margin (or price/variable cost ratio) is that portion of revenue left after direct (or variable) costs have been covered, which can then be applied to fixed costs for the period. Direct costs per unit (or total direct costs) are subtracted from the price (or total revenue) to arrive at the contribution margin (or unit contribution):

$$\text{Contribution margin} = \text{price} - \text{direct cost per unit}$$

or

$$\text{Unit contribution} = \text{total revenue} - \text{total direct costs}$$

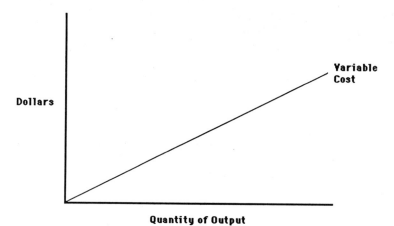

Figure 8.2. Variable cost chart.

Normally, it makes no sense to produce and sell any product or service whose direct manufacturing costs cannot be recovered by the selling price. You can avoid these costs by not producing the unit. Fixed costs, however, are incurred in any case—there is virtually nothing you can do about them. Any unit contribution margin covering fixed costs will be helpful— any excess of price over unit variable costs (direct costs) will go first toward covering fixed costs. Money remaining after fixed costs are covered is profit.

The Break-Even Point

The break-even point is found with the following formula:

$$\text{Break-even quantity} = \frac{\text{fixed costs}}{\text{price} - \text{variable costs}}$$

Altering any element of this equation will affect the results—increasing or lowering your fixed costs, your price, and/or your unit variable costs will change the quantity needed to break even. See Figs. 8.3, 8.4, 8.5*a* and *b*, and 8.6*a* and *b* for graphs of break-even analysis.

Your marketing- and production-mix decisions influence your break-even point. The number of alternative marketing and production mixes that you can consider using is limited mostly by your organization's ability to generate data (especially market and sales-potential estimates) and process them.

Suppose that you have developed a new product or service whose production will require an additional $80,000. If the economic lifespan of the product or service is five years, this original amount represents annual fixed costs of $16,000. Assume that the produce or service share of general overhead amounts to $25,000 per year and variable costs per unit are $12. Your break-even formula appears as:

$$\text{Break-even quantity} = \frac{16,000 + 25,000}{P - 12}$$

where P represents various price levels for your product or service. Since you may want to test price effects at various levels of demand, you could change the quantity and price together:

$$\text{Profit before taxes} = \text{quantity} \times (\text{price} - \text{direct costs/unit}) - \text{fixed-costs}$$

$$= \text{quantity} \times (\text{price} - \$12) - \$41,000$$

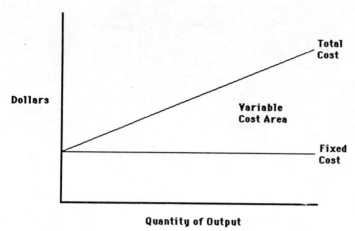

Figure 8.3. Total cost chart.

Raising your price (everything else staying the same) lowers your break-even point, provided demand behaves as expected. If the market behaves as expected at the higher price, you can reduce your risk — fewer units are needed to sell to cover costs. The higher the level of total costs, the higher the quantity needed to cover costs.

Break-even figures are not unalterable; they are the results of your decisions and are thus subject to management control. Basically, your break-even point is determined by your fixed costs, your unit variable

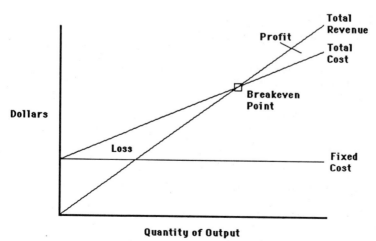

Figure 8.4. Cost-volume-profit (break-even) chart.

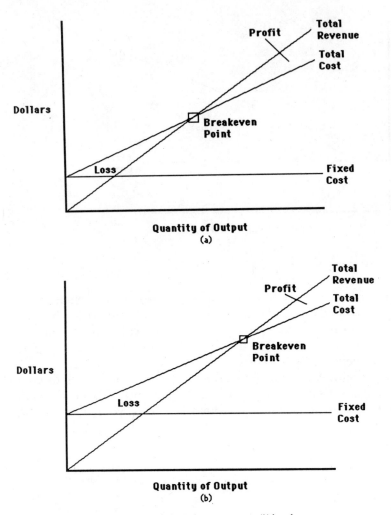

Figure 8.5. (a) Break-even point before plant expansion; (b) break-even point after plant expansion.

costs, and your price. (The demand level is largely out of your control but can be manipulated somewhat by advertising, sales, and sales promotion expenditures).

Lower the Break-Even Point

Depending on your particular situation, you may find that having a high break-even point is too risky — perhaps demand is likely to fall or competition may steal away some of your potential sales. There are three basic ways that you can adjust your break-even point downward:

- *Lower Your Fixed Costs* You may want to try to lower your fixed costs. You could decide that the overhead allocation or actual fixed expenditures should be reduced. Or your assets might have a longer life than first expected (you might be able to use equipment longer than you had believed you could). Perhaps you can use different production techniques that require less fixed investment (but more variable costs may be required).

- *Cut Direct Cost per Unit* Labor-saving approaches may enable you to bring down your unit variable costs. If fixed costs per unit change only

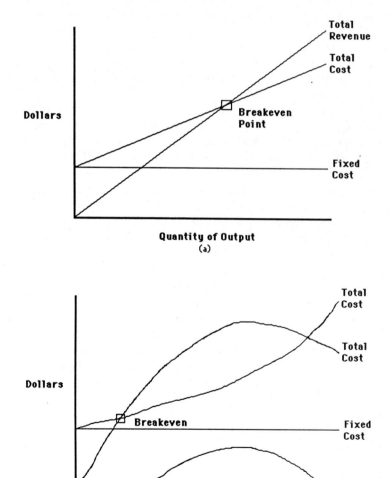

Figure 8.6. (a) Linear cost-volume-profit (break-even) chart; (b) nonlinear cost-volume-profit (break-even) chart.

slightly, you can cut your total costs and shrink the break-even quantity needed.

- *Raise Your Price* Costs notwithstanding, you might feel that your market will accept a higher price for your product or service. Revenue and profits will increase if costs are the same and demand increases even slightly. (Of course, demand could be very price-sensitive, and you could end up with lower revenue and profits.)

The possibilities for changing the break-even point are endless, and the various PricePlan worksheet programs can help you a lot. Many factors need to be taken into account when choosing your marketing mix and trimming your costs. CVP analysis is only one element of input into your pricing decision-making process, but it is a very valuable one. Without its factual basis to guide you, your decisions may be "hit-or-miss" propositions. CVP analysis helps you improve your chances of success by making sensible, goal-directed management possible.

Measurement and control of the break-even point is one of the most important financial tools available to you. It is often neglected when times are good and sales volume is well ahead of the break-even point. If business drops off sharply, the break-even point may seem very high and keeping it high may seem risky. If the break-even point is high and revenue falls drastically, profit can go negative quickly because high fixed costs must still be covered, even though revenue is falling. Your break-even point can safely increase substantially over time as your level of production expands to meet a growing market demand, but it must be monitored on a regular basis.

An increase in the break-even point may not be noticed, and its impact may not be understood. Performing CVP analysis with PricePlan worksheet programs provides you with an increased awareness of the effects of price, revenue, and costs on bottom-line profit. It allows you to take control of your organization's marketing and production economies, rather than having your situation control you. Figure 8.7 lists typical fixed and direct expenses by cost center. Once you have identified relevant costs, you can use PricePlan to analyze cost and profit behavior. An example of this appears in Figs. 8.8 and 8.9.

Performing Cost-Volume-Profit (Break-Even Analysis)

You can easily use CVP analysis to determine how many product or service units you must sell in order to earn a certain level of profit. Using PricePlan worksheet programs, you will get quick estimates of revenue and cost behavior at different selling prices and volume and at varying levels of expenditures for production, distribution, promotion, and other activities needed to sell your product or service. You can easily change these variables and instantly see how many units must be sold to break even or to earn a certain level of profit or surplus.

The PricePlan worksheet programs help you to quickly calculate a break-even point for a product or service. First determine by sales forecasting and other marketing analysis methods the range of units that most likely will be sold during a planning period. Then estimate what costs and revenues will result from selling a quantity within this range. Simply input this information into the worksheet you choose by following the simple instructions given in the program. The programs include Fixed Cost, Single Price; Variable Cost, Variable Price; Product Combinations.

It is important to get accurate forecasted estimates of price and costs from your accounting, finance, production, and marketing departments. Get accurate sales forecasts from marketing and sales departments if you can. Some of these items will change in the near term, so you can use different amounts in your analyses and work up a schedule of possible costs, revenues, and unit demand quantities. It is important to rerun an analysis to handle a range of estimates, and you should rerun an analysis as soon as significant internal or external changes (or indications of change) appear.

Operating Leverage

Leverage explains how you are able to achieve a large percentage increase in profits with only a small percentage increase in sales and/or assets. Operating leverage is tied in with the cost structure of your organization. Organizations with high fixed costs and low per-unit variable costs have great operating leverage. Operating leverage is lowest when fixed costs are low and per-unit variable costs are high. Operating leverage, then, is a measure of the extent to which fixed costs are being used and how sensitive income is to changes in sales.

The degree of operating leverage existing at a given level of sales is

$$\text{Degree of operating leverage} = \frac{\text{contribution margin}}{\text{net income}}$$

The degree of operating leverage is a measure, at a given level of sales, of how a percentage change in sales volume will affect profits.

$$\text{Case 1:} \qquad \frac{\$80,000}{\$20,000} = 4$$

$$\text{Case 2:} \qquad \frac{\$137,000}{\$\ 17,000} = 8.06$$

	Fixed expense	Direct expense
Research		
Marketing research	X	X
Product research	X	X
Product engineering		X
Production Overhead		
Equipment maintenance		X
Repair parts	X	
Supervision	X	
Depreciation	X	
Overtime expense		X
Energy costs	X	X
Sales and Marketing		
Commissions		X
Salaries	X	
Travel and lodging	X	X
Promotion (per period)	X	
Coupons, premiums, rebates		X
Telephone and mail	X	X
Depreciation	X	
Distribution		
Warehouse labor	X	
Supervision	X	
Drivers' wages		X
Workers' compensation	X	
Depreciation	X	
Paid delivery		X
Administration		
Executive salaries	X	
Staff salaries and wages	X	X
Legal and consulting	X	
Public relations	X	X
Supplies	X	X
Insurance	X	X
Interest expense	X	

This example was adapted from Tucker (1980). Please note that these classifications usually vary widely from one organization to another, so the examples given here should not be taken too literally.

Figure 8.7. Examples of fixed and direct expenses by cost center.

For a given percentage change in sales the first case yields a fourfold increase in net income and the second case yields an eightfold increase. The degree of operating leverage is greatest near the break-even point and decreases as sales and profits rise as shown in Table 8.1.

A 10 percent increase in sales increases profits by only 18 percent if sales

Product or project: Radio
Planning period: 1985
Fixed costs: $1000
Direct costs/unit: 0.40
Price/unit: 1.60

Quantity	Revenue	Total costs	Cost/unit	Profit	Profit/unit	Operating leverage
100	$ 160	$1040	$10.40	$-880	$-8.80	-0.14
200	320	1080	5.40	-760	-3.80	-0.32
300	480	1120	3.73	-640	-2.13	-0.56
400	640	1160	2.90	-520	-1.30	-0.92
500	800	1200	2.40	-400	-0.80	-1.50
600	960	1240	2.07	-280	-0.47	-2.57
700	1120	1280	1.83	-160	-0.23	-5.25
800	1280	1320	1.65	-40	-0.05	-24.00
833	$1333	$1333	1.60	$ 0	0	13.50
900	$1440	$1360	1.51	$ 80	$ 0.09	13.50
1000	1600	1400	1.40	200	0.20	6.00
1100	1760	1440	1.31	320	0.29	4.13
1200	1920	1480	1.23	440	0.37	3.27
1300	2080	1520	1.17	560	0.43	2.79
1400	2240	1560	1.11	680	0.49	2.47
1500	2400	1600	1.07	800	0.53	2.25
1600	2560	1640	1.03	920	0.58	2.09
1700	2720	1680	0.99	1040	0.61	1.96
1800	2880	1720	0.96	1160	0.64	1.86
1900	3040	1760	0.93	1280	0.67	1.78
2000	3200	1800	0.90	1400	0.70	1.71

Figure 8.8. Cost-volume-profit (break-even) analysis: fixed costs, single price.

Product or project: Test
Planning period: 1985

Price	Unit sales	Direct costs/unit	Contribution margin	Period fixed costs	Breakeven units	Total profit	Operating leverage
$70.00	50	$ 6.00	0.91	$5000	78	$-1800	-1.78
65.00	100	10.00	0.85	5000	91	500	11.00
60.00	150	9.33	0.84	5000	99	2601	2.92
55.00	200	9.25	0.83	5000	109	4150	2.20
50.00	250	9.60	0.81	5000	124	5100	1.98
45.00	300	10.50	0.77	5000	145	5350	1.93
35.50	400	15.63	0.56	5000	252	2948	2.70
30.00	450	21.78	0.27	5000	608	-1301	-2.84
25.00	500	33.10	-0.32	5000	-617	-9050	0.45

Figure 8.9. Cost-volume-profit (break-even) analysis: variable costs, variable price.

Table 8.1. Relationship of Degree of Operating Leverage to Sales and Profits

Sales	$ 80,000	$ 100,000	$150,000	$200,000
Variable expenses	55,000	65,000	80,000	110,000
Contribution margin	25,000	35,000	70,000	90,000
Fixed expenses	35,000	40,000	40,000	40,000
Net income	$(10,000)	$(5,000)	$ 30,000	$ 50,000
Degree of operating leverage	−2.5	−7.0	2.33	1.8

are $200,000. A 23.3 percent increase in profits occurs at the $150,000 level.

Knowing your operating leverage provides you with a tool to quickly indicate what the impact will be on profits at various percentage changes in sales, without having no prepare detailed income statements. The effects of operating leverage can be dramatic. If you are near your break-even point, small increases in sales can yield large increases in profits.

Margin of Safety

The margin of safety is the excess of sales over break-even sales. It is the amount by which sales can drop before losses begin to occur. The formula is

$$\text{Margin of safety} = \text{total sales} - \text{break-even sales}$$

or

$$\text{Margin of safety \%} = \frac{\$ \text{ margin of safety}}{\text{total sales}}$$

If two companies have the same sales and net income amounts but different cost structures, the company with the higher fixed costs will incur losses more quickly if sales drop off. If the margin of safety is low, you may want to try to reduce fixed costs or increase the contribution margin. The margin of safety can point out a problem in your cost structure and is automatically calculated in the various PricePlan CVP worksheet programs.

As an example of the margin of safety concept, consider Table 8.2.*

*See Garrison, Chapter 6.

Table 8.2. The Margin of Safety Concept

	Company 1		Company 2	
	Amount	%	Amount	%
Sales	$200,000	100	$200,000	100
Variable expenses	150,000	75	100,000	50
Contribution margin	50,000	25	100,000	50
Fixed expenses	35,000		85,000	
Net income	$ 15,000		$ 15,000	
Break-even point	$140,000		$170,000	
M/S dollars	$ 60,000		$ 30,000	
M/S percent	30%		15%	

9
International Pricing

An international organization must develop pricing systems and pricing policies that address the same fundamental factors that exist in each national market in which it operates. The system must also be consistent with uniquely international constraints. Along with the basic dimensions of pricing, international managers are confronted with government tax policies, dumping legislation, resale-price-maintenance legislation, price ceilings, and general governmental review of price levels.

Other international pricing factors include high transportation costs, numerous marketing intermediaries, and multinational accounts demanding equal price treatment regardless of location. A major effect of conducting international business is to lower prices. One of the major reasons for a country to trade internationally is to take advantage of the impact of foreign competition upon national price levels and upon a nation's inflation rate.

Within an international marketing organization, there may be conflicting price objectives. Each manager is concerned about pricing at a particular level, with the director of international marketing seeking competitive prices in world markets. The tax manager must be concerned about compliance with government transfer-pricing legislation, and the company legal counsel must be aware of the antitrust implications of international pricing practices. Of course, there also remains the conflict between production and marketing objectives found in any business organization.

With divergent and conflicting interests combined with the limitations of measuring demand, it is difficult to determine optimal prices in international markets. It is hard to do this in domestic markets and is harder still with international marketing complications. In order to manage pricing effectively in international marketing, an international manager needs to be knowledgeable about factors affecting pricing decisions and possible frameworks for approaching those decisions.

Export Pricing

Cost-plus pricing is often used by exporters to set prices. The cost-plus formula for international marketers would include

1. Manufacturing costs
2. Administrative costs
3. Research and development costs
4. Overhead costs
5. Freight forwarding costs
6. Customs charges
7. Distributor margins
8. Profit allowance

When all these factors are added up, a final price is reached which is often way out of line with competitive conditions in export markets around the world.

The cost-plus pricing method, as you learned in Chapter 2, has several serious problems. First, it completely ignores demand and competitive conditions in target markets. Also, it is often based upon distorted measurements or estimates of costs. In addition, prices are based on costs, which are based on sales volume, which is based on costs.

The cost-plus pricing method is justified only if the cost of information about demand and the administrative cost of applying a demand-based pricing policy do not exceed the profit obtained by using these approaches. The alternative approach is to view pricing as a major strategic variable that can contribute toward achieving key marketing objectives, such as achieving higher market share, increasing short-term or long-term return on investment, or temporarily setting prices low to keep competitors from entering the market.

Costs are, of course, important, but effective export pricing strategies must recognize competitive prices. Competitive prices can be determined only by examining price levels for alternative products available in target market locations. If these price levels have been established, your base price can be determined by doing the following:

1. Estimate quantities purchased at various prices.

2. Estimate incremental and full costs to achieve projected sales volumes.

3. Select the highest profit-contribution price.

You can determine the base price only after evaluating all elements of the marketing mix. Marketing channel lengths and characteristics will affect the final prices, and product costs incurred when adapting to target market requirements will affect the cost base.

Finding the right price level can be extremely difficult in practice. Demand estimation must account for product appeal, and product appeal may need to be measured in experimental settings and test markets. This can be costly and is subject to error. In some international markets, the market potential is too small to justify even the most basic marketing research of this kind, so demand estimates must be based upon the opinions of internal organization and trade personnel. Sometimes demand estimates for target markets can be extrapolated from actual sales in markets felt to be similar to target markets.

Most organizations have estimates of full production costs. Incremental costs are not normally available, however. To get incremental costs, it is necessary to analyze production operations to identify fixed and variable costs. When production can be expanded without increasing fixed costs, variable costs are the only additional costs.

Selection of the most profitable price depends upon the time period of estimation. Beyond the short term, pricing decisions must be based upon all costs incurred over the planning period. These decisions must also acknowledge potential competitive and governmental responses. Because these variables are complex, many organizations pursue secondary objectives rather than the ideal profit-maximization goal.

Price Escalation via Transportation Costs

Increase in an international product factory price, as transportation, duty, and distributor margin increase, constitutes price escalation. Shipping charges, port charges, and insurance charges can add up rapidly when shipping goods overseas. When the total delivered price becomes too high, an international marketer must appraise the extent and nature of the charges and factor them into the pricing formula or select alternative transportation methods. If longer distribution channels or ones with higher operating margins are used, markups can easily exceed half of the total of factory cost plus insurance and freight.

An international marketer can fight this problem by identifying lower-cost merchandise sources, which could include manufacturing or distribution at locations where lower freight and duty charges exist. Selecting more cost-effective marketing intermediaries in the target country or eliminating them altogether can also help to keep prices down.

Dumping Regulations

Dumping is the unfair trade practice of price cutting in order to injure, destroy, or prevent establishment of competition in a country. It can include importing at prices either below those of domestic goods or below those in the exporting country. The General Agreement on Tariffs and Trade defines dumping as the difference between the normal domestic price and the price goods have as they are leaving the exporting country.

Dumping legislation is sometimes used to protect local businesses from predatory pricing by foreigners, and it may be used to limit foreign competition in general. Presumably dumping is harmful to manufacturers and the economy in the importing country, but it does provide a low-cost source of a product for importers. Dumping practiced by individual companies is unpredictable and cannot provide a reliable basis for economic planning even if it does result in injury to domestic suppliers.

In order for the U.S. government to declare a positive dumping occurrence, both price discrimination and injury to domestic business must be present. Existence of either of these alone is insufficient. One way for suppliers to avoid dumping is to differentiate their products from those supplied domestically in the target market, perhaps by offering different options or accessories. Another way is to use nonprice competitive adjustments, such as extending credit, with distributors and other marketing agents.

Currency Devaluation or Revaluation

If the value of one country's currency falls relative to that of another country, the first country's currency is said to have been *devalued*. Some countries experiencing persistent trade deficits attempt to restore equilibrium in their balance of payments by currency devaluation.

When a devaluing country's domestic prices are unaffected by a currency devaluation, the prices of all goods to foreigners fall. As a result of devaluation, in practice the rise in the cost of imported goods raises some costs and prices in the devaluing country, so that part of the intended devaluation effect is reduced. Any price adjustments after a devaluation should take this price inflation into account. When imports are a large percentage of a country's GNP, the price effect of devaluation may be immediate.

Any business selling in a country that has devalued its currency must estimate the price elasticity of demand for its products as well as its basic marketing position. Sales might increase when price falls, but perhaps by less than the amount of the price reduction. This would mean that revenue after the reduction would be less than before the reduction, and demand would be said to be price-inelastic.

If there is a price reduction and demand is price-elastic, devaluation can help an exporter increase profits immediately by raising gross margins, by reducing prices in foreign markets (of course hoping to increase profits as sales increase), or by increasing marketing efforts in product design, distribution, or advertising and sales promotion.

Revaluation refers to an increase in the value of one currency with respect to another. The effect on an exporter or seller in the revaluing country is to decrease the prices of imports and increase the price of exports to foreigners. The marketer must decide whether to pass the price increase on the customers, absorb the price increase and reduce expenses, absorb price increases in foreign currency by reducing prices in the home country, or maintain expense levels and accept lower margins.

Transfer Prices

When an organization is highly decentralized, it can monitor separate operations as profit centers, and it can use transfer prices to monitor, evaluate, and motivate division managers, as well as allow them pricing flexibility.

Transfer pricing systems expanded across national boundaries create complications. Several environmental factors should be considered before transfer pricing is initiated, including

1. Market conditions
2. Buyers' ability to pay
3. Competition presence
4. Deposit requirements on foreign imports
5. Profit transfer rules
6. Joint venture conflicting objectives
7. Taxes
8. Duties
9. Tariffs

Alternative approaches to transfer pricing include

1. Transfer at direct cost

2. Transfer at direct cost plus expenses

3. Transfer at market prices

Some organizations transfer at or near direct manufacturing cost because sales of foreign divisions contribute to corporate profitability via manufacturing economies of scale. Most, however, use cost-plus pricing with the belief that sales of foreign divisions must earn profits at each stage in the organizational system. This will result in a lack of market orientation, because prices are completely unrelated to those of the competition and to the ability of buyers to purchase.

Market-based transfer pricing derives price from those prices set by competition in foreign markets. The constraint is cost, but there exists considerable variation in the definition of costs. An economist would probably suggest that when variable costs are covered by a sale (in the short term, at least), a seller should take the contribution to overhead rather than reject it. Contribution margin is cash that helps to pay for fixed costs. If a given sales transaction not only generates enough revenue to cover direct costs associated with a product but also some additional margin that can contribute toward fixed costs, then the sale is better than no sale at all.

Market-based transfer prices and foreign sourcing of goods can be used to enter a market too small to support local manufacturing, enabling the seller to become established in the market. The seller is then in a better position to decide when to increase commitment to selling in that location. The key to such a strategy is market-based pricing, because without it manufacturing in the local market is the only way to enter that market.

Sometimes income taxes can be minimized by shifting earnings to low-tax locations. Governments have responded to this possibility by attempting to maximize their tax revenues, and the result is a conflict between marketers and governments. Companies must comply with government regulations on the sale of

1. Raw materials

2. Production component parts

3. Finished goods

4. Loans

5. Services

6. Use of tangible property

7. Use of intangible property

When a corporation operates across national boundaries, transfers are subject to review and are examined by tax authorities whose interest is in conflict with that of the seller. Tangible property transfers must also be accepted by customs authorities. Government interest in high import prices to maximize taxes raises local company income, thus income tax revenues.

Company Constraints. Trying to minimize tax payments by transfer pricing can result in distortions of reported company revenues and profits. Some reported profits may be the result of artificially low transfer pricing into low-tax areas and artificially high transfer pricing out of these areas to operating divisions in higher-tax areas. The profit-and-loss statements will show distortions from reality, so this must be taken into account in the organization's monitoring and control systems.

Duty and Tariff Constraints. Organizational costs and profits reflect rates of import duties. The higher the duty, the more desirable a low transfer price. A high duty creates an incentive to keep transfer prices low. Low income tax rates, on the other hand, create upward pressure on prices to shift income away from high-tax areas.

Government Controls. Cash deposit requirements are often imposed on importers. This means that a seller has to tie up funds in a non-interest-bearing deposit for a period of time in order to be allowed to import foreign goods. When this occurs, there is an incentive to minimize the price of the imported product. Transfer profit rules restrict the conditions under which profits can be transferred out of a country. Other controls can include investigating and changing pricing practice in specific industries. For instance, if a local industry is performing poorly, the government may raise the minimum price a seller can charge. The U.S. steel industry has been protected in this manner by U.S. steel price supports.

Multinational Pricing

An *ethnocentric* pricing policy is one which requires that the price for an item be uniform around the world and that customers absorb freight and import duties. This is extremely simple because no competitive or market information is required. An ethnocentric pricing policy is favored by companies who prefer to pay no more than a certain price for a product regardless of where it might be purchased. However, this method does not respond to the competitive and market conditions of each nation and thus does not maximize profits in each area.

A *polycentric* pricing policy permits subsidiary or affiliate companies to set whatever price they want to set. There is no requirement that prices be coordinated between countries. This approach is sensitive to local market conditions, but it allows buyers to take advantage of price differences when local market prices exceed transportation and duty cost differences between markets. Purchasing can be done in low-price markets and selling in high-price markets in a process called arbitrage. Under such a policy, knowledge and experience concerning effective pricing strategies are not applied to each local pricing situation. These strategies are ignored because local managers can price at will and may not be aware of company experiences.

The *geocentric* pricing policy neither fixes a single price worldwide nor ignores subsidiary pricing decisions, but takes a middle position. The assumption is that there are unique local market factors that should be acknowledged, including local costs, income levels, competition, and marketing strategies. A company might pursue a market penetration strategy and price using export sourcing to establish a market. Or the company could supply the target market from higher-cost external suppliers rather than build new facilities. If the price and product are accepted in the market, local manufacturing can be established; if not, other prices can be tried without further commitment.

When you select a price, you must recognize local competition. When pricing consumer products, you must consider local income levels. Some market income conditions may indicate that maximum profitability will be gained by abandoning normal margins. In international marketing, more so than with domestic marketing, there seems to be no such thing as a normal margin. Options such as product-line pricing, where lower-than-normal margins are taken on some products and higher margins on others, can be used to maximize the profitability of the product line and of the entire organization.

Price must fit with the other elements of the marketing program, so price coordination is often necessary at the organizational level. Optimal multinational pricing is determined by comparing the difference between sales and costs for each alternative pricing method. The highest-gross-margin approach might prove less profitable than some other choice because of costs. Any alternative program must be judged in light of its potential costs as well as its projected gains.

10
The Economics of Price and Cost Functions

In the long run, prices must cover costs if a seller is to remain successful, but every product or service need not cover its own cost. The concepts of short- and long-run cost clarify how prices and costs are related.

Short-Run Cost Functions

If you know your minimum cost to produce each quantity of product or service output, you can define a cost function to show how various types of costs are related to output. Your organization's cost functions may vary in the short and long run. In the short run, you cannot vary quantities of fixed resources used. These fixed costs determine your scale of operations. In the short run, the following three costs are particularly important.

Total fixed cost is your total expenditure per time period for fixed production inputs. The quantity of fixed inputs is unvarying over production volume (by definition), so the total fixed cost will be the same whatever your level of sales volume. (You *can* change fixed costs, but only by a very major change in your investment in plant and equipment.)

Total variable cost is your total expenditure on variable inputs per time period. Higher output rates require use of a greater quantity of variable inputs, which means higher cost. Up to a certain output rate, total variable cost increases at a decreasing rate; beyond this rate, total variable cost increases at an increasing rate.

It is important to understand this decreasing rate of marginal return on cost. At small output rates, increases in the utilization of variable inputs may bring about increases in their productivity, causing total variable cost to increase with output, but at a decreasing rate. Beyond a certain point, there are diminishing marginal returns from the variable input, and total variable costs increase at an increasing rate.

Total cost is the sum of total fixed cost and total variable cost. To obtain your total cost at a given output, just add total fixed cost to total variable cost at that output. The total cost and total variable cost functions differ by the total fixed cost. See Fig. 10.1 for an illustration of total cost curves.

Average Costs in the Short Run

You care about the average cost of a given product or service as well as the total cost incurred. Average cost tells you how much an item costs per unit of output. There are three average-cost functions, one for each of the three total-cost functions (see Fig. 10.2 for graphs):

Average fixed cost is total cost divided by your organization's output. Average fixed cost must decline with increases in output, since in that case it equals a constant (total fixed cost) divided by the increasing output rate.

Average variable cost is total variable cost divided by output. At first, increases in the output rate result in decreases in average variable cost. Beyond a point, however, increases in output result in higher average variable cost. As more and more variable inputs are utilized, the extra output produced declines beyond some point, so the amount spent on variable input per unit of output tends to increase. See Table 10.1 for an example of the decrease and eventual increase in average variable cost.

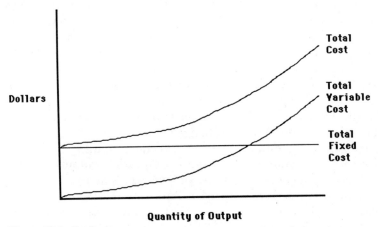

Figure 10.1. Total cost curves.

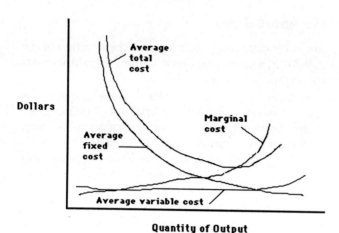

Figure 10.2. Average cost curves.

Average total cost is total cost divided by output. At any level of output, average total cost equals average fixed cost plus average variable cost. If, as the output rate goes up, both average fixed cost and average variable cost decrease, average total cost must decrease, too. Beyond some point, however, average total cost must increase because increases in average variable cost eventually more than offset decreases in average fixed cost. Average total cost achieves a minimum later than does average variable cost, because increases in average variable cost are, for a time, more than offset by decreases in average fixed cost.

Table 10.1 is an example (adapted from Mansfield) of calculated values of average costs:

Table 10.1. Relationship between Output and Average Variable Cost

Units produced	Average fixed cost	Average variable cost	Average total cost
1	$30,000	$ 800	$30,800
2	15,000	700	15,700
3	10,000	700	10,700
4	7500	720	8220
5	6000	760	8760
6	5000	800	5800
7	4286	860	5146
8	3750	1000	4750
9	3333	1600	4933

Marginal Cost in the Short Run

Marginal cost is the addition to total cost resulting from the addition of the last unit of output. Table 10.2, a continuation of Table 10.1, shows marginal cost in relation to output and total cost levels.

When output is between zero and one units per day, marginal cost is $800, since this is the extra cost of producing the first unit. The marginal cost, $800, is the difference between the total cost of producing one unit ($30,800) and the total cost of producing 0 units ($30,000).

Marginal cost will vary, in general, depending on your organization's output level. In the previous example, marginal cost is $600 when production is between one and two units, $1000 when production is between five and six units, and $6400 when production falls between eight and nine units. Marginal cost, after decreasing with increases in output at low-output levels, increases with further increases in output. If, beyond some point, variable cost increases result in less and less output, a larger and larger quantity of variable inputs must be added to produce another unit of output. It becomes more and more costly to produce each extra unit as output rises.

The relationship between marginal cost and average cost is important. The marginal-cost curve intersects the average-variable-cost curve and the average-total-cost curve at their minimum points. If the extra cost of a unit of output is greater (or less) than the average cost of units of output already produced, addition of an extra unit of output must raise (lower) the average cost of production. If marginal cost is greater (less) than average cost, average cost must be rising (falling). Average cost can be at its minimum only when it equals marginal cost. The same is true for average total cost and average variable cost, in both the short and the long run (see Fig. 10.3a and b).

Table 10.2. Relationship between Martinal Cost, Output and Total Cost

Units	Total cost	Marginal cost
0	$30000	$ 0
1	30800	800
2	31400	600
3	32100	700
4	32900	800
5	33800	900
6	34800	1000
7	36000	1200
8	38000	2000
9	44400	6400

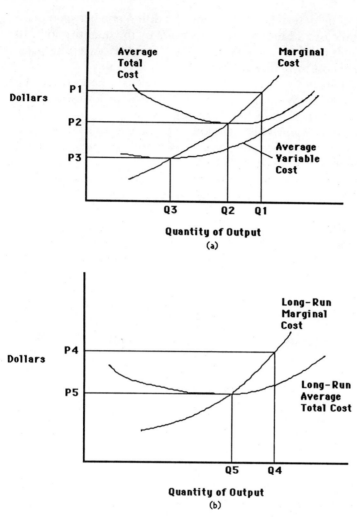

Figure 10.3. (a) Prices, quantities, and costs in the short run; (b) prices, quantities, and costs in the long run.

Pricing in the Short Run

In the short run, your profits can be maximized by setting price equal to marginal cost. At this point on your cost curve, profits are maximum because a lower price causes a high sales volume, with accompanying incremental costs which will eventually exceed price gains; a higher price produces a lower sales volume, and profit is lower. As long as price exceeds marginal costs, your profits can be improved by increasing your output.

Your profit can be determined by taking the difference between price and average total cost and multiplying this value by the quantity sold. In the face of competition, you may be forced to lower price, setting price equal to marginal cost to realize the most profitable output.

Under short-run competitive conditions, two prices are important. The lowest price you can charge and still recover all costs is the lowest point on your average-total-cost curve, where marginal cost equals average total cost. The other important price is at the lowest point on your average-variable-cost curve. Here, the price fails to cover average total costs, and a loss occurs when the item is sold.

At prices higher than the minimum average variable cost, some funds are contributed toward covering your fixed costs. Any price lower than the minimum average variable cost causes losses of out-of-pocket revenue in excess of your direct product or service costs, so price should be equal to or greater than the average variable cost (unless you are selling the item as a loss leader to help sell more profitable items in your line).

Long-Run Average Cost

Your long-run average-cost function shows your minimum average cost of producing each output level, i.e., when any desired scale of production capability can be established (see Figs. 10.4*a* and *b*). This cost pertains to a period long enough that all inputs are variable and none is fixed. Consider it your planning horizon: you must be continually planning ahead and trying to decide upon strategies in the long run.

If you are able to establish production capability in any of several ranges, you should choose that capacity which has the lowest cost. You should choose a small capacity if you feel that demand will be low in the long run and medium or high capacity appropriate to meet long-run forecasted demand levels. Long-run average cost tends to decrease as more and more output is produced over time, so you might want to plan for some excess capacity at the beginning.

Returns to Scale

What determines the slope of your long-run average-cost function and those of your competitors? The shape of a particular long-run average-cost function must necessarily depend upon the characteristics of the production function — whether there are increasing, decreasing, or constant returns to scale.

Suppose you increase the amount of production assets and expenses by

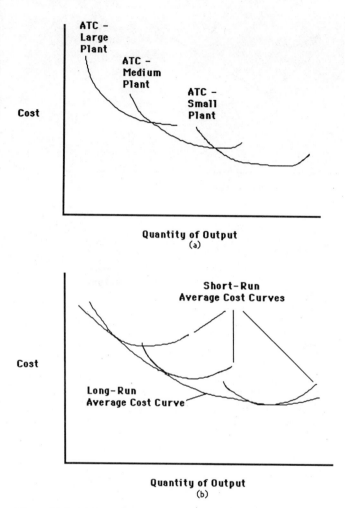

Figure 10.4. (a) Short-run average cost curves; (b) long-run average cost curves.

the same proportion. What happens to your output? If your output increases by a larger proportion than each of the inputs, you experience *increasing returns to scale.* If your output increases by a smaller proportion than each of the inputs, you get *decreasing returns to scale.* When output increases by the same proportion as each input, you have *constant returns to scale.* See Fig. 10.5 for an illustration of the three types of returns to scale.

Your organization may be more efficient than two of your competitors whose combined output is at the same total capacity as yours, because you may be able to utilize certain techniques that smaller organizations cannot.

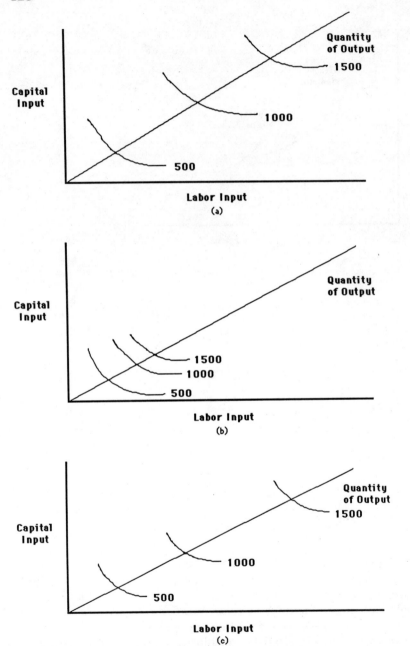

Figure 10.5. (a) Constant returns to scale; (b) decreasing returns to scale; (c) increasing returns to scale.

Greater specialization can also result in increasing returns to scale. As you use more equipment and people to perform a certain activity, it may become possible to subdivide tasks and allow various inputs to specialize.

As your organization grows, you can expect problems of coordinating activities and conveying information promptly and accurately to multiply. Decreasing returns can then set in.

Whether you get increasing, decreasing, or constant returns to scale depends on your range of output. There might be increasing returns to scale up to some level of output, constant returns to scale up to a higher output level, and from then on, decreasing returns to scale. In any event, you can expect long-run average cost to rise eventually, due to the expenses of coordination problems, increased bureaucracy, and reduced flexibility.

Pricing in the Long Run

In the long run, you have the opportunity to adjust your production capacity. Therefore, all of your costs are variable in the long run. A price should be set to maximize profits, as in the short run. Long-run losses indicate a declining market or unnecessarily high cost, and a shift in strategy can often solve loss problems.

Long-run profits are maximized by setting price equal to long-run marginal cost (until competition becomes stiff). The lowest price that you should charge in the long run is at the point where your long-run marginal costs equal your long-run average costs. This is equal to short-run average cost and short-run marginal cost.

The Experience Curve

Some successful organizations have taken a different pricing approach, utilizing the experience cost curve. With the experience cost curve, unit cost declines with cumulative volume over time as a seller develops versions of the product or service with lower costs. The increasing costs of higher volume are offset by experience and more efficient production methods.

The classical profit-maximization criteria are not applied here. Instead, strategic pricing over the product or service life cycle is used. A product or service is introduced at a price high enough to recover committed research and development costs. Unit costs are high at this time, but the organization anticipates that an experience cost curve will exist over the life cycle of the product or service.

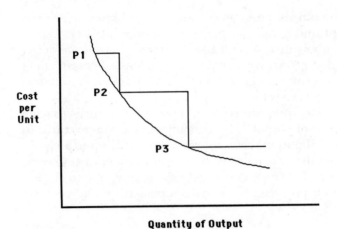

Quantity of Output

Figure 10.6. Pricing and the experience cost curve.

The experience cost curve can be used as an effective planning tool to forecast what costs are expected to be as time progresses and sales volume accumulates. Prices can be lowered over time if sufficient volume can be generated. An organization will develop a long-run marketing plan involving price and nonprice strategies to produce needed volume. Price may be lowered over time, depending on the break-even volume and price (see Fig. 10.6). Price reductions, plus well-planned promotions, expand sales volume substantially. Manufacturers of hand-held and pocket calculators, as well as makers of electronic watches, seem to have used such a strategy successfully.*

* Sources for this section include Mansfield (1977 and 1982), Hirschleifer, and Bell.

11

Issues in
Price Planning

Pricing and the Profit
Maximization Objective

Is Pricing the Dominant
Focus of Business?

If you are to maximize profits, you must set a price such that your marginal revenue equals your marginal cost. This means that you must, at a minimum, estimate demand at all price levels and marginal costs at all sales volumes, and you must estimate the extent to which demand is related to cost incurred by advertising and other marketing expenditures.

Analysis of this sort is incredibly difficult to perform, so it is rarely tried in practice, as studies of actual pricing practice seems to verify. How can you accurately estimate demand for a product or service even at a single price? Most pricing emphasis is on building a "normal" price. Rather than trying to perform elaborate demand and cost analyses, most business managers use a much simpler process.

First, an estimated cost is built up, including direct costs, a share of indirect costs, and a satisfactory profit margin. Next, it is guessed whether an adequate sales volume can be obtained at a price based on the estimated cost. Then competitive pressures and strategic issues are considered. Finally, the price is arrived at.

The profit margin may be varied as circumstances permit, and the cost can sometimes be changed. The starting point is a price based on total cost as derived from conventional cost accounting, not a price based on marginal cost. The reasoning used is that if each product or service contributes significantly to covering overhead costs and profit, a satisfactory profit will be made on the total of all products or service items.

Profit arrived at by this method will probably not be the same as the maximum profit possible when using prices computed from economic analysis, but the price-setter can feel more confident about the probability of obtaining this profit figure than she or he might be about relying on the estimates used with the marginal approach.

Pricing does not seem to be the dominant focus of business enterprises that the economists suggest. Pricing is but one element of a total marketing mix which includes product design, packaging, distribution, merchandising, personal selling, advertising, sales promotion, and product service and support. If the only relevant costs to the pricing process are marginal costs, then cost allocations of depreciation, overhead, and other joint costs to products or services are probably useless or too complicated. Some economists suggest that cost accounting is useless for pricing (I do not agree), but scores of business organizations have cost accounting systems that do allocate costs to products and services.

Inconsistencies between Profit
Maximization Theory and Practice

There are quite a few differences between the profit maximization objective and actual business practice. One is the practice of giving donations to organizations and individuals outside the business. The rationale for donations is that they will create a more favorable climate for the business in the community, which seems consistent with the idea of long-run profit maximization, but then why do charitable contributions decline during economic recessions?

Some organizations give discharged employees generous severance pay. Some business managers do not spend very long hours at work. Many corporations have plush offices and large expanses of land just for show. Cost-cutting programs are often implemented, even though costs are supposedly as low as possible already. These are just some of the many examples of how businesses do not seem to place profit maximization at the top of the list of organizational objectives.

If it is true that in the long run all costs are incremental costs, then long-run profit-maximization prices are consistent with full-cost pricing. The long-run profit-maximization costs are estimates of future replacement costs, while conventional costs deal with current costs. The two approaches result in the same prices only when the market is static and in perfect equilibrium.

Business pricing policies and practices do not seem to be consistent with other maximization objectives: welfare maximization, satisfaction maximization, minimax (a method for getting the best performance out of the worst possible conditions), or other economic concepts that attempt to describe a maximizing theory for business. The pricing practices of business organizations do not seem to follow any one maximization objective but rather seem to try to balance out several objectives.

Should Businesses Even Try to Maximize Profit?

The Ethical Problem.   Profit maximization requires that managers think solely of the best interests of the business owners, but the interests of all parties having a stake in the business must be taken into account. Profit maximization requires that executives use every way possible to keep wages and employee benefits down, to get the most money from buyers, to sell only the lowest-quality products customers will buy, to ignore community responsibility, and so forth.

Business managers, like any other people, do not act in ethical isolation. Naturally they are often concerned with matters of conscience involving their employees, their families, and their communities. Managers cannot be concerned with a wide variety of ethical issues and at the same time work solely to maximize the financial objectives of the stockholders.

Social and Legal Pressure.   A variety of international, federal, state, and local laws indicate to businesses that society disapproves of pure profit maximization. A business executive could not legally maximize profit even if he or she wanted to. Economists often assume that business people are completely knowledgeable, rational, and amoral, but modern theories of markets assume that businesses and consumers are not purely economic in nature.

Areas of pricing that lead to a potential conflict with society include

1. Horizontal price fixing
2. Minimum price-level setting
3. Vertical price fixing
4. Price discrimination

Horizontal price-fixing agreements between competitors at the same level in the marketing channel (also known as collusion) are illegal, regardless of how reasonable the resulting prices may be. The Sherman Antitrust Act and the Federal Trade Commission Act address this issue and allow the U.S. government to extract extensive legal damages penalties from offenders.

For sellers to require retailers to sell branded products for a particular list price (depending upon state laws) is a form of fixing minimum price levels. The Miller-Tydings and McGuire Acts prohibit this.

For a seller to charge competing customers different prices for similar products is a form of vertical price fixing as well as price discrimination. The Robinson-Patman Act prohibits it, unless the price differences are based solely on costs and not on differences in market power, i.e., the ability to force sellers to offer goods or services at a lower price than buyers pay. Some states have passed laws requiring certain minimum prices, to protect small firms from predatory pricing by large businesses.

It is in your organization's best interest for you to be knowledgeable about existing federal, state, and local legislation affecting your pricing practices. You should obtain good legal advice when you aren't sure where you stand. It is also beneficial to pay close attention to ethical pricing-practice restraints, because social pressures for ethical behaviors that exist now might become future laws.

Problems with Price Setting

Price Elasticity and Price Levels

For any product or service, in either the long or short term, there is a demand function relating price to the quantity demanded. If there is perfect competition, the price tends to be at or near the industry marginal cost, and under pure monopoly the price will be at the point where industry marginal cost equals industry marginal revenue. Demand will be more elastic under monopoly than under competition. The more inelastic the demand curve is, the greater will be the gap between the competitive and monopoly prices.

It is often stated for some products that cost increases can be passed on to customers because demand is inelastic. This may be true, but an elasticity value is only valid for one particular price. As the price rises, elasticity rises because product substitutes become more and more attractive to buyers. A monopoly price will be set at or near the point where the product demand is so elastic that it destroys opportunities for profitably raising prices further. This point represents the price ceiling. The gap between the competitive and the monopoly prices forms the possible range of price control in the industry.

If price is outside the range of industry price control, the market is out of balance, with strong forces driving the price back into this range. Inside the range there is usually some degree of unbalance, too. If price is above the purely competitive level, it is also above marginal cost, and there is a temptation for sellers to drop price to gain profitable incremental sales volume. On the other hand, if price lies below the point where marginal revenue equals marginal cost, there is a temptation for sellers to band together into a cartel to raise the price. The problem for you as an individual seller is to locate the price position where you are and where your industry is.

Finding the Real Determinants of Demand

You need to know the real determinants of cost and of demand. Both cost and demand information are important, but the two are very different. Knowledge of costs is based on past experience and can often be reduced to rules of thumb. Basic demand determinants, describing how and why customers will purchase various products at various prices, can rarely be easily analyzed. Most managers can make reasonable estimates of what the effects of changes in unit costs or level of output will be, but they cannot do the same for effects of price on demand.

Even an astute monopolist would have some difficulty recognizing a price zone of increasing price elasticity of demand. There is a good likelihood that she or he would accidentally go too far in changing prices and have to backtrack. To make matters worse, there is the possibility that the demand curve would shift to the left unpredictably, making a price change quickly become obsolete. The closer a price gets to the pure monopoly price, the more vulnerable it is to shifts in the demand curve.

Price movements always begin with fringe buyers, not average buyers. A given buyer may have numerous uses for a product, with different product substitution options for each use. For many needs, out of the scores of ones filled by the product, how will other products be substituted if the price is raised too high? When fringe buyers (those first willing to change) begin substituting other products for yours, you should study how and why the substitution is taking place. This will help you decide early whether the price should be adjusted or the product (along with delivery and customer service) should be modified.

Variations in Elasticity

There are often significant differences in short- and long-term elasticity, because many factors are involved. Demand tends to be more elastic when viable product substitutes are available, when a luxury item is involved, or when the price equals a large portion of a buyer's budget. When there are few if any product substitutes available, when the product is a necessary item, or when the price is low compared with the purchasing budget, product demand tends to be less price-elastic.

Some studies have shown that the life cycle of the product (or, more specifically, of the brand) affects the price elasticity of demand observed.

Price elasticity tends to be decreasing during product introduction, growth, and maturity and increasing during product decline. This is often the basis for a market-penetration pricing strategy.

Pricing and Promotion

You should coordinate your pricing strategy with all aspects of your marketing strategy, including promotion. Promotion is used to communicate with people and to convince them to buy from you. Potential buyers should be made aware of your prices in order to be influenced to buy from you. Pricing information can be effectively transmitted to potential purchasers by promotion. Department and discount stores, furniture stores, grocery stores, and appliance stores all use promotional media extensively to announce price levels and changes.

Promotion can be used to increase sales. Effective promotion messages and efficient use of media can enable you to sell more items at the same or higher prices. Higher prices are often possible because through promotion messages buyers become more aware of and (hopefully) more interested in unique product or service characteristics that induce them to buy.

Effective promotions can alter the shape and position of your market-demand curve, changing price elasticity. Hopefully, your promotional efforts will cause demand to become less elastic (less price-sensitive) by reinforcing differentiating product or service features and impressions of quality. When you develop new markets for items, promotion may actually be directed toward increasing price elasticity of demand. If long-run economies of scale exist, a penetration price can be used to open up a large market. This assumes that potential buyers will respond to lower prices (demand is price-elastic). Promotion can make demand more elastic by improving awareness and desire for substituting the new product or service for established ones.

Promotional Support for Price Strategy

Promotion activities include all types of marketing activities designed to stimulate demand. Four categories of such activities are advertising, publicity, personal selling, and sales promotion activities.

Advertising involves communication of messages to selected large audiences using impersonal means to inform and influence people about a product or service offered for sale. This might include radio and television commercial broadcast messages or newspaper and magazine advertisements.

Publicity refers to communication of information by personal or impersonal means that is not directly paid for by the sender of the message. Public relations, the marketing part of publicity, involves news releases for new products and services that can be published by editors in newspapers and magazines or broadcast in news programs on radio and television.

Personal selling is tailored to a specific person or a small group of people and involves personal contact. Sales promotion includes all methods of stimulating demand that do not fit easily into the above categories, and it is used in conjunction with personal selling (for example, when personal selling is utilized, direct-mail or telephone selling could be used, too).

Sales promotion activities can include contests, premiums, coupons, trading stamps, printed and audiovisual displays, sampling, catalogs, product demonstrations, tie-in promotions, and special deals. A consumer contest could be held at the same time as a contest for dealer sales people. Or a premium could be offered to consumers as a piggyback offer combining two products for a low price. This could be combined with a "dealer loader"—a special-purpose discount offered to the dealer of the product.

The Promotion Mix

The various elements of the promotion plan are combined in the promotion mix, which is a combination of promotional efforts. These elements must work together to achieve the same marketing objectives. Advertising, publicity, personal selling, and sales promotion can be coordinated in a campaign which produces a highly effective and efficient promotional program. It will be easier for you to complete a sales transaction if your customer has been partially or fully presold by your promotional efforts.

Why Promote?

Three reasons for you to promote your products and services are:

1. To communicate your message to potential buyers
2. To convince potential buyers to purchase from you
3. To help you compete against your rivals

Spreading your ideas to others is the main reason why you will want to promote. Communicating ideas is not enough, however. You must be convincing enough to induce potential buyers to purchase from you instead of from your competitors. Promotion provides the stimulation needed to convince consumers or resellers to turn to you. If you have a good product, an efficient marketing channel, and an appropriate price, you still may not have the critical differential advantage over your rivals.

The competitive characteristics of your promotions play a vital role in your marketing strategy.

Promotional Objectives

Numerous promotional objectives could be stated, because promotions can be versatile and the application to a wide variety of organizations is possible. Bell (1979) states a few of the most common promotional objectives:

1. To increase sales
2. To maintain or increase market share
3. To create or improve brand recognition, acceptance, or insistence
4. To create a favorable climate for future sales
5. To inform and educate the market
6. To create a competitive difference
7. To improve promotional efficiency

Should You Promote?

Promotion is not always highly effective or efficient. Whether you should rely heavily on promotion depends on what opportunities you have for promoting your product or service. Bell states the following five key conditions that indicate a favorable opportunity to promote:

1. There should be a favorable trend in demand.
2. There should be strong product differentiation.
3. There should be some hidden qualities in the product or service.
4. Emotional buying motives should exist.
5. Adequate funds should be available.

Summary of Pricing and Promotion

Promotion refers to activities that create or stimulate demand for products and services. The tools used include advertising, publicity, personal selling, and sales promotion. The purposes of promotion are to communicate, convince, and compete, and more specifically, to increase sales, improve market position, and strengthen customer or user awareness and acceptance of a product or service.

Promotion is a crucial link in any strategic marketing effort. Promotional strategies, like pricing, are one of the primary means of communicating your strategy signals and policies to your marketplace. Although pricing and promotion are only part of your marketing mix, they can be the most important elements. For some products and services, price *is* the product. No matter how important it is, however, price alone should not be used to compensate for inferior products, incompetent personnel, or poorly researched and implemented plans.

Although pricing is one of the key ways to communicate your organization's philosophy and strategy signals to the marketplace, it does so indirectly. Buyers may not rank pricing as particularly important. Many will rank convenience, reputation, and service ahead of pricing. Thus it is important for you to research the reasons why buyers do business with you in order to quantify the value that you are providing through the prices you set. Then use promotion wisely to effectively implement your ideas for success in the marketplace.*

Pricing and Marketing Channels

Marketing intermediaries share a common interest in achieving a high sales volume for a product. The burden of obtaining these sales, the profit margins received, and the services required all provide potential sources for marketing channel conflict.

There are several sources of marketing channel conflict involving pricing, including resale price maintenance, the size of functional discounts, and intermediaries' reactions to producer price changes. The producer may want to have brands sold for a particular retail price. If local laws will permit it, the producer may have the legal authority to pressure for retail price maintenance.

Often marketing intermediaries must be persuaded to conform to the producer's desired price. Some will seek higher margins than suggested and thereby charge too much. Others may cut prices, thus threatening the brand's quality image or discouraging other intermediaries from selling this item.

Usually, a producer who seeks to control retail prices must expect to experience stiff resistance from mass-merchandising outlets. Some resellers may refuse to handle a product if it is sold to discounters. The producer must determine which type of marketing channel promises the greatest profits and choose the appropriate resale-price-maintenance policy.

---

*See also Bell, Chaps. 14 and 18, for more details on promotion strategy.

Marketing channel conflict may also affect the discounts given as compensations and incentives to marketing intermediaries. The price-setter must consider the services required of the intermediaries, the support given to them, current industry practices, and the relative marketing power of each member in the marketing channel. If a producer sells under a private label to a powerful wholesaler, he or she must expect to give larger discounts off the list price. A seller of several well-established brands will not need to offer the same price concessions.

When changes in the list price are considered by a producer, changes for marketing intermediaries must be allowed for. Lowering the retail price will lower the value of inventories held by intermediaries, so these resellers must be told in advance that a change is coming, and their prices should probably be adjusted to keep their profit margins adequate. Giving price breaks on future orders will help, but may not be enough. If marketing channel members' needs are not considered when a price change is made, channel conflict will increase and the producer's sales may suffer significantly.

Price Discrimination

Price discrimination refers to the practice of charging different markups over marginal cost to different customers. Although it is illegal to price-discriminate between customers who compete against each other, different prices might legally be charged to noncompeting customers through trade or geographic discounts.

Although charging different prices to different customers might be legal, it is not desirable unless it is profitable, such as when you sell to two or more market segments and the following conditions exist:

1. Customers are separated—geographically or by trade status.

2. Customer demands are of different magnitudes and price elasticities.

3. Reselling by one customer to another is impossible.

If such conditions exist, you can maximize profits by determining your most profitable rate of production. Equate marginal cost and marginal revenue where two markets conform to the above conditions. You as seller must sell your output to the markets in such a way as to maximize profits. Do this by making sure marginal revenue is the same for each market.

Market Segmentation

A market-segmentation strategy involves presenting customers in different market segments with two different simple prices. As stated previously,

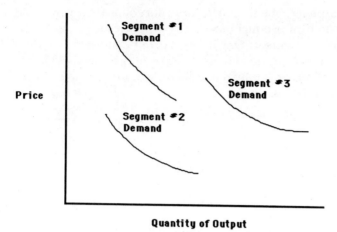

Figure 11.1. Demand curves for three market segments.

this can be accomplished only when the two segments are effectively insulated from each other. If the two segments are not insulated, customers in the low-price segment will be able to earn a profit by reselling to the high-price segment. See Figs. 11.1 and 11.2.

Following the example of Hirshleifer (1976) for monopoly (a strong marketer can act as a monopolist to a certain extent), let AR_1 (Q_1) and AR_2 (Q_2) represent the average revenue functions of two market segments (AR_1 is a function of Q_1, AR_2 is a function of Q_2). The corresponding marginal revenue functions are MR_1 (Q_1) and MR_2 (Q_2). A marginal cost function can be expressed as MC (Q) where $Q = Q_1 + Q_2$.

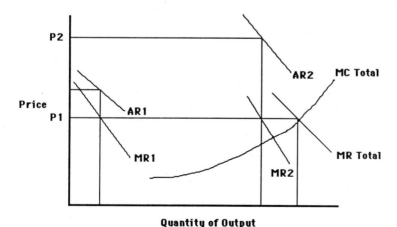

Figure 11.2. Market segmentation with two market segments.

At any level of output Q, whenever MR_1 does not equal MR_2, you would want to reallocate units of product or service output from the low to the high marginal-revenue segment. One optimal profit condition is $MR_1 = MR_2$. You would want to produce more units of output only so long as $MC < MR_1 = MR_2$. Thus, if production is increased, we have as the optimal market segmentation condition:

$$MC(Q) = MR_1(Q_1) = MR_2(Q_2)$$

where

$$Q = Q_1 + Q_2$$

Knowing that $MR_1 = MR_2$, we can say that

$$P_1\left(1 + \frac{1}{e_1}\right) = P_2\left(1 + \frac{1}{e_2}\right)$$

where

$e_1 =$ segment 1 elasticity and $e_2 =$ segment 2 elasticity.
$P_1 =$ price for segment 1.
$P_2 =$ price for segment 2.

If the magnitude of e_1 exceeds the magnitude of e_2 (segment 1 is more elastic), then

$$\left(1 + \frac{1}{e_1}\right) > \left(1 + \frac{1}{e_2}\right)$$

and therefore

$$P_1 < P_2.$$

The segment with the more elastic demand receives the lower price.

Multipart Pricing

A multipart pricing strategy involves a seller's presenting a single price schedule to each customer, so that a relatively high price is charged for initial units up to some given limit, and a lower price is charged for additional units taken later. See Fig. 11.3a, b, and c. The idea is for the seller to capture a portion of the profit that would otherwise go to buyers.

You will not ordinarily be ideally successful at multipart pricing. One reason is that although you might like to offer different price schedules to

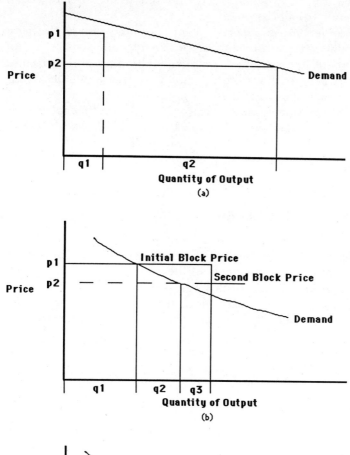

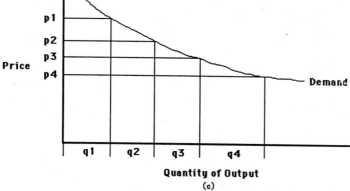

Figure 11.3. (a) Two-part pricing; (b) unsuccessful two-part pricing; (c) multipart pricing.

each different customer, legal and cost considerations may dictate a common price schedule for all customers.

For some customers the initial price-quantity combination on the price schedule is too high — they will not purchase enough units so that they can take advantage of the lower price offered beyond the initial purchase limit. The resulting inability to offer different multipart price schedules to different customers may cut substantially into your profit.

The transaction cost of metering and recording sales for a complex price schedule will be greater than for a one-price schedule. Also, as with market segmentation, it is necessary for you to control transfer of units from low-price to high-price segments.*

The Transfer Pricing Problem

Your organization may be decentralized, with operating divisions staffed by managements who have authority for making decisions independently and who are responsible for a segment of the overall organization profit. The degree of decision-making authority granted to division management varies, but the idea of decentralization is clearly to divide an organization into relatively self-contained divisions and to allow these divisions to operate autonomously.

When division profit is calculated, problems occur if divisions are not completely independent. If one division supplies goods or services to another division, a transfer price must be set in order to calculate the buying division's cost and the selling division's revenue, since revenue and cost are both necessary to calculate profits.

There may be a conflict in setting transfer prices because the information may be used for decision making as well as profit determination.

Market Prices

Using a market price to set transfer prices assumes that a market actually exists at or near the price level in question. Market prices, even if they exist, might be difficult to determine. Market prices may fluctuate. The selling unit may be able to sell at a lower cost to the buying unit than in the open market, because of savings in shipping and marketing costs. If there exists no real market at the price level considered for transfer, it is difficult to determine a price.

If a market price can be found, it is a good measure to use to evaluate

---

* References for this section include Hirshleifer and Bell.

division performance. The market transfer price represents the actual conditions under which divisions would operate if they were separate business entities in the marketplace. Market prices are good for evaluating performance because they are objective and cannot be changed by the seller.

Assume that you have two operating divisions, a producer and a seller. The producer must produce a unit of raw material which can either be sold as soon as it is produced or be transferred (sold) to the seller, where it can be resold at some time in the future.

As an example, if you want to evaluate each of your unit managers, a price of $55 could be used as a transfer price. This is combined with a $43 variable production cost to give a $12 profit. This profit depends on how efficient the producer is and on the ability to produce at the right time for the market.

The seller division should buy from the producer only if the raw material can be stored and sold in the future for a profit. If the seller division buys the material for $55 and sells it 4 months later at $67, incurring interest and storage expenses of $8, the profit earned is $4 as shown in Table 11.1.

The total profit for the organization is $20, but the total profit is divided into producing and selling profits, which can be used to evaluate the division managers' performances.

Negotiated Prices

By using negotiated prices, division managers can set transfer prices through the bargaining process. This can work if:

1. Both buyer and seller can freely transact business outside the organization.
2. Negotiators have complete market information.
3. All transfer prices are actually negotiated between the buyer and seller.

Table 11.1. Market Transfer Price as a Measure of Performance

	Producer division	Seller division
Sales	$55	$67
Cost	43	59
Profit	$12	$ 8

The negotiated price might solve some problems encountered in basing market-transfer prices on list prices or using market prices, both of which ignore the lower costs of selling to a division within the same organization. Managers' (expensive) time can be used in transfer-price bargaining, though, so prices should probably be negotiated only periodically.

Using negotiated prices will likely still leave some problems. The buying division might be able to obtain a lower price in the open market, in which case it could show higher profits by buying outside. The selling unit's profit might decrease in such a case, depending upon its inventory and the strength of demand for its products. As a result, the organization as a whole might experience lower profits. In the long run, the producing division manager would want a lower price to avoid having unused production capacity. If capacity is unused, negotiated transfer prices are better than prices forced upon division managers.

Cost-Based Prices

A transfer price based on variable costs can be useful in making some decisions, but it may result in losses for selling divisions. There may be little or no reason in such a case for the division to sell at these transfer prices. If no market exists, there may not be an alternative, and some cost measure could be used. The divisions could be merged, but this may not always be desirable.

Using full-cost or cost-plus pricing can lead to trouble, too. If these pricing methods lead to prices higher than market prices, the buying division would be better off purchasing outside, which could create excess capacity for the producer division. The variable cost of the producer plus some allocated fixed cost might be higher than market prices, but if the market price is higher than the variable cost alone, the organization as a whole is better off having the producer continue to produce.

Another problem with this approach is that cost determination becomes an issue, especially when costs are allocated. However, using full-cost or cost-plus pricing can motivate the supplier to give good service to the buyer division. Full cost would increase the producer division profit as long as full cost exceeds variable cost and excess capacity exists. The difference between full cost and variable cost contributes to fixed cost, which increases profit.

Decision Making

When operating divisions are dependent upon each other, transfer prices can communicate to managers information to help them make their decisions. Internal prices facilitate transactions just as external prices do. External and internal prices supply information about the prices of the various inputs to production, such as labor, materials, and component parts. Some decisions, for example, the make-or-buy decision, are based on the relative level of these prices.

If divisions are interdependent, division managers need information on when to deal inside and when to deal outside the organization. If the buying division can buy from either source, the buying decision depends on the relative level of internal and external prices.

Decisions must be made about how much to buy and how much to produce, including price and quantity decisions. In a perfectly competitive market, it does not matter where the buying or selling is done. The seller can sell all output on the open market and no excess capacity will exist, so the buyer should be able to purchase anywhere. The selling costs would probably be the same in either case, too.

If a market is not perfectly competitive, market transfer prices are undesirable if the seller is prevented from going outside to find lower prices. The seller must be allowed to lower the transfer price or idle capacity might develop and seller profits suffer. The buyer should purchase internally as long as the selling division's variable cost is below the open-market price. In this case, though, a conflict could arise. A negotiated transfer price might be better. The seller would not allow idle capacity to exist for long, and the market price to the buyer could be negotiated at a low enough level to not encourage outside buying.

Variable Costs

Often variable costs should be used for making production decisions. Costs that change with volume are the relevant costs. The safest transfer price is one equal to variable cost, but this is not very good for evaluating performance.

When pricing and deciding on output levels, the variable cost is again the relevant cost, especially when the markets are not perfectly competitive. If the markets are perfectly competitive, market prices are sufficient to use in determining pricing and output levels. If the producing division produces items that the buying division can buy from the producing division, process further, and sell, the variable cost of processing by the buying division plus the market price for the unprocessed product must be less than the price for the processed product in order to justify processing.

Economic theory tells us that the market price and marginal cost in a perfectly competitive market should be equal. To maximize profit, a division manager should produce and sell until marginal cost equals marginal revenue. In a perfectly competitive market, the demand curve lies horizontally because a producer can sell any level of output at the market price, and marginal revenue and market price are equal. If production is expanded until marginal cost equals marginal revenue, marginal cost will equal market price.

Marginal revenue represents the additional revenue gained from selling one more unit of a product. Marginal cost is the additional cost of producing and selling that unit. If marginal cost remains constant, it represents the variable cost per unit. Variable cost, then, can be used as a measurement of marginal cost.

In an imperfectly competitive market, neither a market price nor a full-cost transfer price is adequate in making pricing decisions. Assume in the following example that the selling division can sell product A to the buying division or in the open market. The buying division can process product A further and sell it as product B. Marginal revenue and variable costs are shown in Table 11.2.

Here a constant variable cost is used as a measure of marginal cost. When you compare the marginal costs and revenues, you see that six units of product B can be sold in the market before the net marginal revenue equals the variable cost of product A, or $30.00. Six units of product A should be sold to the buying division for processing into product B and subsequent sale in the market. Five units of product A can be sold in the market before the marginal revenue equals the variable cost of $30.00, so 11 units of product A should be produced.

The output decision was made using marginal revenue of product A and the net marginal revenue of product B. One unit of product A has a

Table 11.2. Variable Cost as a Measurement of Marginal Cost

Units	Product A		Product B		Product B marginal revenue − product B variable cost
	Marginal revenue	Variable cost	Marginal revenue	Variable cost	
10	$ 5.00	$30.00	$ 10.00	$20.00	$(10.00)
9	10.00	30.00	20.00	20.00	0.00
8	15.00	30.00	30.00	20.00	10.00
7	20.00	30.00	40.00	20.00	20.00
6	25.00	30.00	50.00	20.00	30.00
5	30.00	30.00	60.00	20.00	40.00
4	35.00	30.00	70.00	20.00	50.00
3	40.00	30.00	80.00	20.00	60.00
2	45.00	30.00	90.00	20.00	70.00
1	50.00	30.00	100.00	20.00	80.00

Table 11.3. Marginal Revenue: Internal versus Outside Sales

Units of product A	Marginal revenue if sold outside	Net marginal revenue if sold internally
1	$50.00	$80.00
2	45.00	70.00
3	40.00	60.00
4	35.00	50.00
5	30.00	40.00
6	25.00	30.00
7	20.00	20.00
8	15.00	10.00
9	10.00	0.00
10	5.00	(10.00)

marginal variable production cost of $30.00 and should be sold where profit is highest. The $30.00 production cost is the total additional cost incurred when selling product A in the open market. If product A is processed further and sold as product B, additional processing cost is $20.00 per unit, which should be subtracted from the marginal revenue of product B to get the net additional revenue to the organization.

If the producing division has excess capacity, it can rearrange the above data to show where units should be sold, as in Table 11.3.

Note that for production quantities up to seven units, it pays to sell the product internally to the second division. At seven units, it does not matter where the units are sold. At levels above seven units, the product should be sold in the open market instead of internally.

In imperfectly competitive markets (and most markets are of this type), allocation of costs requires variable cost prices. A market transfer price may cause the second division to restrict its buying, causing the producing division to produce at less than the most profitable level of output. A variable-cost transfer price will be inadequate for evaluating performance, however. A conflict may occur when this data must be used for pricing and production decisions as well.

12

Implementing Pricing Strategy

This book has presented the theory underlying the pricing of products and services, and it has applied that theory to common pricing strategies. In this chapter we can put all of the pricing principles together to create a methodology for implementing pricing in a variety of settings. This book has attempted to give a reasonably complete coverage of the subject of pricing strategy in practice, but you may want to refer to other sources for greater detail. For a more detailed coverage of this subject, refer to the sources listed at the end of the book.

The following steps, many of which closely parallel the steps in strategic planning covered in Chapter 1, outline the basic areas to cover when implementing prices:

1. Determine buyer or user needs, wants, and desires.
2. Conduct an analysis of your external environment and select a grand strategy.
3. Evaluate your competition.
4. Determine your market position relative to that of your competition.
5. Establish a price list for all your products and services.
6. Conduct a complete cost analysis.
7. Develop product-line financial statements.
8. Assess your existing and future operations.
9. Review and modify your operations policies as necessary.

10. Communicate your plans to your employees, distributors, and retailers.

11. Communicate your plans to your buyers or users.

12. Monitor the results of your programs.

13. Make tactical decisions and modify strategies as necessary.

You do not have to follow the order of these steps, but following them in order may reduce your risk of implementing prices improperly. You must become aware of the needs, wants, and desires of people who will buy your products or services before you can develop your marketing mix, including price levels. Also, setting prices before analyzing your competition can be a big mistake. Some of the steps listed above will be discussed below.

Determine Buyer or User Needs, Wants, and Desires

Gathering data on potential and existing buyers and users of your product or service is vital for establishing any pricing program. An analysis of customers, including interrelationships among customers, includes identifying key product-buying or product-using decision makers. Some of this information could be obtained or processed in automated fashion from marketing research firms, trade associations, the federal government, or other sources.

Buyer or user survey sampling can also be performed by randomly selecting groups of people to question about their buying or use habits and intentions for the future. By doing this at random across your market, you can be sure that the results are statistically sound and that the sample results represent the true results for the total market. You can then base your decisions on the sample results. Regardless of how you gather information about your market and target market segments, you must understand your marketplace and develop reasonable buyer or user profiles to guide your pricing actions.

Determine Your Market Position

There are many resources available to help you determine your current market position. An enormous amount of public information is available for all markets. The U.S. Census Bureau collects data for specific markets. Demographic information pertaining to housing, income, marital status, and many other characteristics can often be broken down by census tract and block groups within the marketplace. This will enable you to pinpoint and analyze differences by geographic location.

After you examine the market you are interested in, your own current market position can be determined by conducting various forms of marketing research. More and more organizations of all types, both large and small, are collecting marketing information on attitudes, lifestyles, and product and service needs of existing and prospective customers. This research is collected from secondary sources or primary research conducted by the organization itself, and it can be used to supplement demographic data collected from the Census Bureau.

You will find that market research is extremely important in determining the value that your customers and prospective customers see in your products or services and those of your industry in general. Without this vital information, your entire pricing strategy would be based solely on subjective interpretation.

Evaluate Your Competition

One way you can evaluate your competition is by conducting a shopping survey. This could be done by researchers within your organization or by an outside research service. Some industry trade associations will have useful information available to you, consulting firms sometimes publish pricing data, and an outside advertising agency or market-research firm may be able to obtain key competitive price information for you.

Another way to evaluate your competition is to conduct an analysis of your competitors' financial positions. If financial reports are available to the public, you may be able to analyze the strengths and weaknesses of your competition in areas where potential pricing opportunities may exist.

Establish Price Lists

When establishing prices for all your products or services, you should begin by assigning the task to a group of people who are knowledgeable about all of your products and services. This group should try to focus only on the issues immediately at hand. Try to include people from the following areas of your business:

1. Marketing and sales
2. Finance and accounting
3. Operations and production
4. Policy and planning

5. Training and communications

You can probably think of other areas to represent or modifications of these classifications. The important thing to remember is to include people from all functional areas, because each has an important contribution to make in establishing and maintaining prices.

Marketing brings expertise in areas including product or service design and packaging, distribution, communication and promotion, and pricing. Marketing also brings information concerning customer and marketing-channel relationships. Marketing should also have access to research on the value that exists or that prospective customers attribute to your company and its products and services. Your organization's competitive position is monitored by marketing people, and they have access to considerable amounts of other analytical and descriptive information.

Financial people have expertise in cost and asset and liability management, and they are responsible for cost collection and analysis of fixed or variable product-cost relationships. Interest rates are studied relative to asset and liability management, and the cost of money and funding methods are studied. In short, the finance department monitors all factors which affect the profit position of your organization (even if yours is a nonprofit organization).

Operations and production personnel are responsible for developing and making ready for sale all of your product and service offerings. These people are responsible for scheduling production to meet projected customer demand, and they must be made aware of the purchasing schedules of distributors, retailers, and consumers or industrial or commercial buyers. The production department can relate costs with production schedules in order to help determine the feasibility of changing prices during the upcoming budgeting period.

Your policy and planning people are knowledgeable about your organization's various policies, but be sure that a key decision maker is included in the price-planning group. If you include planning people who are not in the center of policy determination and implementation, the price programs you formulate may conflict with the overall strategies and plans of your organization. Including a top executive familiar with these plans and strategies is crucial.

Personnel who train must have an understanding of your products and services in order to adequately train employees responsible for actually implementing your pricing programs. Training is a key element in communicating pricing information to the marketplace, and training personnel need to have a good understanding of individual employee abilities in order to select individuals who are likely to be most successful in implementing price programs and subsequent price changes.

Communications people are experts in communicating information about your organization's product or service as well as information about pricing to existing and prospective consumers, industrial or commercial buyers, and end users. Communication of vital pricing information might be through advertising, public relations, or sales promotion. Sales representatives will be responsible for any personal selling, but their efforts must be coordinated with any communications designed to be conveyed through impersonal media such as radio, television, printed catalogs, product and price sheets, newspapers and magazines, point-of-sale displays, and product paging.

You can make your price-planning and -implementation group large or small, but the important task is to create an effective list of your products or services and their respective prices, perhaps including upper and lower limits which you plan to keep prices within. Your list will include existing products and services as well as those you plan to introduce, and the list may include products or services which you give away free of charge. Try to assign a perceived value as well as internal cost to you for important items that are offered, even if there is no formal price attached to them.

Generating this price list is a good opportunity for you to periodically reexamine cases where your products or services are being offered free of charge or at low promotional prices. Some promotional items can be given away, but a so-called "self-liquidating" promotion often occurs when an item is offered at or near your cost so that you can continue to supply such an item for a long period of time.

When you have generated your price list, your price planning group could continue with the process and assist with analysis and implementation of prices, or the group could be disbanded and only one or a very few persons could be held responsible for implementing and monitoring your organization's price programs.

The person or small group chosen to implement and monitor price programs would likely be from your marketing area and should have extensive knowledge of your organization, a solid understanding of the many analytical tools used, and superior communications ability in order to present price findings to management, employees, distributors, retailers, buyers, and end users. Having a person from the price-planning group be in charge of price implementation ensures that you will experience continuity in price levels and control over pricing implementation.

Conduct a Complete Analysis of Costs

This book has reviewed many aspects of costs as they influence pricing. Costs must be analyzed so that prices can reflect cost behavior. This will help reduce the risk of low or negative profitability as a result of ignoring costs when setting prices. When you conduct a cost analysis for implementing prices, you should consider costs of all products and services.

Costs can be reviewed in several ways. One would be to review the cost of each item with people inside your organization who have expertise in accounting and cost analysis. Another approach is to hire a consulting firm to analyze your cost picture. Using such an outside service has the advantage that you can learn new ways to identify and monitor costs in relation to prices and profit. Each approach will result in estimating costs of products and services and in creating a permanent procedure to track costs.

You could establish a task group to create a list of products and services and their prices by using subjective methods. This approach is subject to errors, but it can be an easy and quick way to conduct a cost analysis. Whatever method you use, you must get a solid handle on your cost and profit picture in order to be able to implement profitable pricing strategies.

Prepare Product or Service-Line Financial Statements

After you have obtained complete cost information about your products and services, you have one remaining important component for determining product or service profitability. Revenue generated by product and service items will round out the profit picture. Cost and revenue data can be aggregated by product or service line or by specific item. If your organization is large, including transfer prices between operating units, interest charges, and overhead allocation will make this process difficult.

You may find that detailed product or service-line financial reports are not necessary for some products which generate little or no revenue. Also, you may have limited resources and expertise to develop detailed product or service-line financial statements. You must, however, consider creating product or service-line financial statements in order to assess the contribution each item is making to your organization's profitability.

Assess Your Existing and Future Operations

The operations capability of your organization may constrain your pricing programs. This capability includes the capacity and capability of your information management systems, manual bookkeeping systems, and data collections systems. Even the most powerful computer-based information system is subject to certain constraints, such as changing the system to handle new product or service configurations.

Your information system may be unable to handle some forms of pricing, especially if you use a sophisticated pricing which requires that customer accounts be analyzed in detail. You will need to review the capabilities of your information system in order to determine what constraints it creates for changing prices.

Your manual record-keeping systems are likely to be even more constrained than is a computer-based one. The time required to complete necessary paperwork may more than offset any extra revenue generated from this work. You need to assess the ability of your people to handle manual input of price information when you consider any price adjustments.

Review and Modify
Operations Policies

You have probably already established policies for your various product and service items, but over time these guidelines may have become forgotten or out of date. When you make a price change, your customers may insist on having you adhere to your already established policies. You need to identify current and past policies and to conform with procedures that you have already communicated to distributors, retailers, and buyers and users of your products and services.

Policies can be changed, but any change must be done in light of past policies and the future effects of any adjustments. Policies and procedures, like objectives and strategies, should be periodically reviewed to ensure that they are not forgotten and that they remain effective.

Communicate to Employees,
Distributors, and Retailers

Ultimately, the control you have over your price implementation rests with employees and others who deal directly with your customers. These people must be totally supportive of any price changes you may make. Lack of proper training of these people or failure to communicate properly to them the purpose of a price adjustment can seriously damage the effectiveness of the price change.

It is essential for someone to explain to key employees and marketing agents why a price has been changed and what the probable impact will be. When these people are made part of the decision-making process, they will be more highly motivated to implement your programs and may be able to directly improve your profitability. Training can be used as a powerful motivator, but lack of it can devastate a pricing program.

One way to motivate people to support a price change program is to use performance-based incentives and bonuses. Tying incentives to a pricing increase can increase revenue and decrease costs. Programs should be monitored to ensure that the level of customer service is kept high, but in total, incentives, bonuses, and commissions tied to pricing programs can provide effective means to assist you in price implementation.

Communicate to Buyers and Users

Communicating to the buyer and user is just as important as communicating to your staff and marketing agents. An improperly communicated price change can cause enormous resentment and even lose business for you. Price change communications to buyers and users should be kept short, especially if prices are to increase. Try not to emphasize prices, but rather focus on quality, service, or rapid delivery. If you build a case for higher prices, buyers will not be reluctant to purchase from you.

Monitor Results

Monitoring results can be the most difficult step in any price-implementation program. Monitoring is difficult because you must collect information from employees and marketing agents who deal directly with customers and users. Collecting this information is time-consuming and subject to error, but if you implement price changes without tracking the effects, you lose vital information about your customers and their reactions to your policies.

If a price change is not doing what you had hoped, the only way you can improve results is by knowing about the true impact of the change through monitoring. You can monitor pricing effects by surveying your customers, employees, and marketing agents, or you can analyze changes in revenues, costs, and the resulting profits. Just make sure you manage to track the results.

Summary

The importance of the role of nonprice factors has been increasing in the marketing process, but price remains an important and challenging element. When you set a price, you must pay attention to your pricing in theoretical economic models, which suggest how you can find short-run profit-maximizing prices when demand and cost estimates are available.

The theory, however, leaves out some factors that you need to consider in actual pricing situations, such as

1. The presence of other objectives
2. The presence of multiple parties—buyer, seller, governments, competitors
3. Marketing-mix interactions
4. Demand estimate uncertainties
5. Cost estimate uncertainties

In practice, you may orient your pricing toward:

1. Cost (markup and target pricing)
2. Demand (perceived-value and demand-differential pricing)
3. Competition (going rate and bidding pricing)

When you consider changing your established prices, you must carefully consider your customer or user and competitor reactions. Price elasticity of demand summarizes probable buyer reactions. There are several ways to estimate price elasticity of demand and some problems in interpreting it, but it remains a key factor in determining how much can be gained (or lost) by price changes.

Take your competitors' reactions into account. These depend heavily upon the nature of the market structure and degree of homogeneity (similarity) of products or services. Competitive reactions may be studied to see if they flow from a set reaction policy or from a new assessment of each challenge.

If you initiate price changes, you must consider probable reactions of suppliers, marketing intermediaries (distributors, agents, retailers), and governments. If you face a competitive price change, you must try to understand the intent and probable duration of the change. When you need to act swiftly in response, you should still preplan your possible reactions to different potential price developments.

Price planning and management is complicated. Various products or services in a line usually have important demand and cost interrelationships. Your objective should be to develop a set of prices that maximizes profits on your whole line and for your entire organization. You can develop tentative prices for products and services by marking up costs (full, incremental, or conversion) and modify these prices by individual market factors (demand, competition, government regulations).

Various planning systems and tools available from KM Software Solutions can be of great help to you when deciding what your options are and what the consequences of certain actions will probably be. Each situation is, of course, unique, but this pricing guide should help you to make many better-informed, more-profitable pricing decisions in the short and long term.

National Association of Accountants
919 3d St., NW
Washington, DC 20006

Planning Executives Institute
5500 College Corner Pike
Oxford, OH 45056

References

In this book, you have been introduced to some of the tools which can make price planning in your organization more effective. These tools can provide you with an objective to aim for and a measuring scale with which to monitor your efforts. The following references are some of the many sources available for further information on price and profit planning.

These references are highly recommended — all were used as sources to a certain extent. I have tried to acknowledge all major adaptations from these sources at the end of each section where they are used. A list of professional and business associations is also provided. These may be contacted for additional information on this subject.

Alpert, Mark I. *Perspectives in Marketing Management.* Glenview, Ill.: Scott, Foresman & Company, 1971.

Anthony, Robert N. in *Price Theory in Action,* ed. Donald Stevenson Watson. Boston: Houghton Mifflin Company, 1965.

Bell, Martin L. *Marketing Concepts and Strategy.* Boston: Houghton Mifflin Company, 1979.

Bower, Marvin, *The Will to Manage: Corporate Success through Programmed Management.* McGraw-Hill, New York, 1966, pp. 17 – 18. (Also referenced in Pearce and Robinson, p. 5.)

Cox, William E., Jr. *Industrial Marketing Research.* New York: John Wiley & Sons, 1979.

Dilworth, James B. *Production and Operations Management,* New York: Random House Business Division, 1983.

Garrison, Ray H. *Managerial Accounting: Concepts for Planning, Control, Decision Making.* Plano, Tex.: Business Publications, 1982.

Guiltinan, Joseph P., and Paul, Gordon W. *Marketing Management: Strategies and Programs.* New York: McGraw-Hill, 1982.

Hirshleifer, Jack. *Price Theory and Applications.* Englewood Cliffs, N.J.: Prentice-Hall, 1976.

Hughes, G. David. *Demand Analysis for Marketing Decisions.* Homewood, Ill.: Richard D. Irwin, 1973.

Keegan, Warren J. *Multinational Marketing Management.* Englewood Cliffs, N.J.: Prentice-Hall, 1974.

King, W. R. and Cleland, D. I. *Strategic Planning and Policy.* New York: Von Nostrand Reinhold, 1979.

Kotler, Philip. *Principles of Marketing,* 3d ed., Englewood Cliffs, N.J.: Prentice-Hall, 1986.

Lilien, Gary L. and Kotler, Philip. *Marketing Decision Making: A Model-Building Approach.* New York: Harper and Row, 1983.

Mansfield, Edwin. *Microeconomics.* New York: W. W. Norton & Co., 1982.

Mansfield, Edwin. *Principles of Microeconomics.* New York: W. W. Norton & Co., 1977.

Moebs, G. Michael and Moebs, Eva. *Pricing Financial Services.* Homewood, Ill.: Dow-Jones Irwin, 1986.

Moore, Carl L., Jaedicke, Robert K., and Anderson, Lane K. *Managerial Accounting.* Cincinnati, Ohio: South-Western Publishing Co., 1984.

Oxenfeldt, Alfred R. *Pricing Strategies.* New York: American Management Associations, 1975.

Paley, Norton. *Pricing Strategies and Practices.* New York: American Management Associations, 1983.

Pearce, John A. II and Robinson, Richard B., Jr. *Strategic Management: Strategy Formulation and Implementation.* Homewood, Ill.: Richard D. Irwin, 1982.

Stacey, Nicholas A. H. and Wilson, Aubrey. *Industrial Marketing Research.* City: Hutchinson and Co., Year.

Symonds, Curtis W., *Pricing for Profit.* New York: American Management Associations, 1982.

Tucker, Spencer A. *Profit Planning Decisions with the Break-Even System.* New York: Thomond Press, 1980.

Webb, S. G. *Marketing and Strategic Planning for Professional Service Firms.* New York: American Management Associations, 1982.

Wheelright, Steven C. and Makridakis, Spyros. *Forecasting Methods for Management.* New York: John Wiley & Sons, 1977.

Wind, Yoram. *Product Policy: Concepts, Methods and Strategy.* Reading, Mass.: Addison-Wesley Publishing Co., 1982.

Woelfel, Charles J. *Guides for Profit Planning.* Washington, D.C.: Small Business Administration, 1975.

Wolfe, Harry D. *Business Forecasting Methods.* New York: Holt, Rinehart & Winston, 1966.

Professional and Business Associations

American Accounting Association
653 S. Orange Ave.
Sarasota, FL 33577

American Institute of Certified
  Public Accountants
666 Fifth Ave.
New York, NY 10019

American Institute of Management
125 East 38th St.
New York, NY 10016

American Management Association
135 West 50th St.
New York, NY 10020

American Marketing Association
250 S. Wacker Dr.
Chicago, IL 60606

Institute of Internal Auditors
5500 Diplomat Circle
Orlando, FL 32810

Glossary

Absorption costing: A type of product or service costing which assigns fixed production costs to the units produced as a product cost. Contrast with direct costing.

Accounting profit: Total revenues minus total costs.

Activity ratios: Measures of the effectiveness of asset management.

Antitrust laws: Federal laws designed to eliminate monopolies and restraint of trade.

Assets: Economic resources that are expected to benefit future business activities.

Average fixed costs: Total fixed costs divided by the number of units produced.

Average variable costs: Total variable costs divided by the number of units produced.

Average total costs: Total costs divided by the number of units produced.

Break-even analysis: Study of the relationship of revenues, costs, and profits (also called cost-volume-profit analysis) in order to find the point at which revenue just covers costs.

Break-even point: The point at which total revenue equals total cost.

Budget: A specific plan that shows how an organization or business unit will spend money over time in order to meet its goals.

Business risk: The risk of bankruptcy or variability of profit arising from the type of business activity conducted.

Cash discount: A discount for payment of a debt in advance of a due date.

Clayton Act: An act passed in 1914 to outlaw price discrimination (charging different prices for a product if the effect might be to reduce competition).

Competition: The effort of two or more sellers, acting independently, to attract customers by offering the lowest price, the highest product quality, etc.

Competition-based pricing: Pricing based on the prices charged by competitors for similar products or services.

Complements: Products that are used and/or purchased together.

Contribution margin: Selling price minus variable unit costs.

Cost allocation: Assigning one or more cost items to one or more segments of an organization according to benefits received, responsibilities, or some other measure of use.

Cost-based pricing: Pricing in which the costs of doing business are added up and used as a basis for setting prices.

Cost of goods or services sold: Cost of merchandise or services that are acquired and resold.

Dealer: One who purchases goods for resale to final consumers.

Degree of operating leverage: The percentage change in net operating income divided by the percentage change in output or sales.

Demand-based pricing: Setting a price with respect to buyer expectations and needs.

Demand forecast: A prediction of future sales of a product or service.

Devalue: To reduce the value of a country's currency in terms of other currencies.

Direct costing: Product or service costing which charges fixed production costs immediately against the revenue of the period in which it was incurred, without assigning it to specific units produced (also referred to as variable costing).

Econometric models: Mathematical economic models used to make economic forecasts and to suggest economic policy by measuring the impact of one economic variable on another.

Economies of scale: A decrease in average cost that is associated with an increase in volume or output.

Elastic demand: A demand function for which a percentage change in price is met with a larger percentage change in the quantity demanded in the opposite direction.

Expenses: Expired costs that are deducted from revenue for a given period.

Exports: Goods or services that are sent by one country to another.

External information: Information that comes from sources outside an organization (from the external environment).

Financial leverage: The magnification of changes in earnings available to owners resulting from changes in net operating income.

Financial ratios: A group of ratios used to test and measure the financial status of an organization.

Fixed costs: Costs that do not change with changes in the level of production within a relevant range of output.

Foreign exchange rate: The rate at which one currency can be exchanged for another.

Goods: Tangible products.

Gross margin: Sales minus cost of goods or services sold.

Import duties: Taxes paid on foreign products entering the domestic market.

Imports: Goods or services that are bought by one country from another country.

Income statement: A record of the money an organization receives and pays out (also called a profit and loss statement).

Inelastic demand: A demand function for which a given change in price will be met by a less than proportionate change in the quantity demanded in the opposite direction.

Inflation: An increase in the volume of money and credit relative to available goods and services, resulting in a rise in the general price level. Each unit of currency is thus worth less and prices go up.

Internal information: Information that comes from the various departments of an organization (from the internal environment).

International business: The conduct of economic activity across national borders.

International trade: The exchange of products and services by nations through exports and imports.

Law of supply and demand: The economic law that states that the price of a product or service is determined by the interaction between the amount of the product or service supplied by producers and the amount demanded by consumers or users.

Leverage: The magnification of profits and losses resulting from the use of fixed costs.

Leverage ratios: Measures of an organization's fixed-charge financing.

Liabilities: Debts of an organization and claims on its assets. Also, the debts and obligations of an individual or business.

Liquidity: The ability of an organization to meet financial obligations or liabilities without having to convert fixed assets to cash or otherwise endanger the financial condition.

Liquidity ratios: Measures of an organization's ability to meet cash obligations.

Management: The process of making plans that will achieve the goals of an organization and of directing people as they execute these plans.

Management information system: The methods by which an organization supplies its managers with information that is needed to make business decisions.

Marginal cost: The cost of producing one additional unit of output.

Marginal revenue: The revenue received from selling one additional unit of output.

Market demand: The total volume of a product or service that would be bought by a defined customer group in a defined geographical area in a defined marketing environment under a defined marketing program.

Market development: Seeking increased sales by selling existing products in new markets.

Market segmentation: Identifying distinguishable segments of a market consisting of buyers with different needs, buying styles, and responses to variations in product or service offerings.

Market penetration: Seeking increased sales for existing products and services in existing markets through more aggressive marketing effort.

Marketing: Business activity directed at satisfying customer needs and wants.

Marketing channel: The set of suppliers, distributors, agents, and retailers that distribute a product or service.

Marketing mix: The set of controllable variables that an organization can use to influence buyer responses (product, place, promotion, and price).

Marketing research: Research that provides the information on which product or service design, production, distribution, promotion, and price are based.

Market segmentation: The process of sorting consumers or users of a product or service into groups based on similarities with groups and differences between groups.

Markup pricing: Pricing in which a set percentage is added to the cost of producing the product or service.

Monopoly: A situation where only one seller exists for a good or service.

Net operating income: Income before interest and taxes produced by operating assets (assets, net of depreciation and bad debts, employed in the ordinary course of the business).

Net profit: Sales minus cost of goods or services sold, minus operating expenses, minus income taxes from operating profit.

Nonprofit corporation: A private corporation formed for charitable or educational purposes, and which aims to earn zero profit (neither a surplus nor a deficit) in the long run.

Objectives: Statements of basic purpose and mission to guide an organization to what it should try to accomplish with various activities in the external environment.

Operating costs: Cost of goods or services sold plus operating expenses.

Operating leverage: The magnification of changes in net operating income resulting from changes in sales or output.

Operating margin: Net operating income divided by sales.

Operating profit: Sales minus cost of goods or services sold, minus operating expenses.

Organizational demand: An organization's share of market demand.

Period costs: Those costs being deducted as expenses during the current period without having been previously classified as product costs.

Planning: Setting goals for an organization and deciding how these goals should be met.

Price: The amount of money a seller requires a consumer to pay for a product or service (the list price). The market price is the price that a buyer is actually willing to pay.

Price differentiation: Differences in price that depend on differences in cost, as distinct from price discrimination, which is not a function of costs but rather a function of relative elasticities of demand.

Price discrimination: Discrimination among classes of demanders with different elasticities of demand. Charging a higher price to those with relatively less elastic demands than to those with relatively more elastic demands.

Price elasticity of demand: The price responsiveness of the demand for a good or service, defined as the percentage change in quantity demanded divided by the percentage change in price.

Price fixing: An agreement by two or more sellers to charge the same price for a product or service.

Price lining: Setting prices for several products or services at the same time.

Primary demand: Demand for a new product or service.

Product: Something offered to a potential buyer for attention, acquisition, or consumption. This can consist of a physical object (a good), a service, a personality, a place, an organization, or an idea.

Product development: Seeking increased sales by developing improved products for existing markets.

Product item: A specific instance of a product; a product in a product line.

Product life cycle: The distinct stages in the sales history of a product, from introduction, to growth, to maturity, to decline.

Product line: A group of products closely related to each other by, e.g., satisfying a need, being used together, being sold to the same customers, being marketed through the same channels, or being priced in the same price range.

Product mix: The combination of all products offered by a seller.

Profit: The part of revenue that remains after paying for materials, supplies, labor, and capital funds supplied to generate the revenue.

Profitability ratios: Measures of management's ability to generate profits.

Promotion: Any business communication which persuades a person or organization to purchase a product or service. It includes advertising, public relations, sales promotion, and personal selling.

Psychological pricing: Pricing in which break-off points (e.g. $12.99 or $10.95) are used or products are sold in groups (e.g., 3 for $5.00) in order to make the buyer think that he or she is getting a better deal.

Pure competition: A type of competition in which a large number of sellers offer the same product at the same price.

Pure monopoly: A type of market situation in which only one seller supplies a particular product or service, for which there exist no close substitutes, and thereby controls the price.

Quantity discount: A discount from the list price based on the size of an order.

Rate of return: Profit on a percentage of the original cost.

Ratio analysis: The use of various ratios (such as asset turnover) for comparison with the ratios of the same organization earlier in time or with those ratios of other organizations to establish the progress or deterioration of financial position as to liquidity, profitability, etc.

Regulation: The establishment of rules or laws by governments in order to control business activities.

Resale price maintenance: A system whereby the manufacturer stipulates a specific retail price and the retailer is not allowed to sell the product at a lower price.

Retailers: Individuals or businesses that perform all of the activities involved in selling products or services directly to end users or consumers.

Return on investment (ROI): The money earned on an investment of capital funds.

Risk: Exposing money to the chance of loss in the expectation of earning a return on investment. Risk may consist of business risk, financial risk, market risk, interest rate risk, or purchasing power risk.

Robinson-Patman Act: An amendment to the Clayton Act that was passed by the U.S. Congress in 1936. Its purpose is to ensure that all businesses that buy from the same supplier pay the same prices.

Sales forecast: An estimate of dollar or unit sales during some future period of time.

Secondary demand: Demand for one organization's product or service in preference to those offered by competitors.

Semivariable costs: Costs that contain both fixed and variable elements.

Services: Products that consist of the use of a person's skills or abilities to satisfy the needs or wants of the buyer.

Sherman Antitrust Act: An act of Congress, passed in 1890, that outlawed combinations of businesses (trusts) and other practices that limit competition.

Skimming: Charging a high price for a popular product or service until competitors enter the market and drive the price down.

Strategic planning: Planning that usually takes place at the top-management level and which consists of setting goals, deciding upon policies, and planning the future direction of an organization. It is also referred to as long-range planning.

Surveys: A way of gathering data that involves interviewing potential buyers or users of a product or service, or asking them to complete questionnaires.

Subjective probability: An opinion about the likelihood that a given event will occur.

Tactical planning: Planning usually performed by middle and first-line managers, also called short-range planning. Tactical planning consists of making decisions about how to run an organization on a day-to-day basis, deal with problems, meet specific goals, and execute programs.

Target market: The segment of the market that is most likely to buy a given product or service.

Target pricing: Pricing based on the desired return on investment. The seller finds out what amount of money must be received in order to meet costs and how it must be received in order to yield the desired return on investment. Then the price is set accordingly.

Tariff: A government-imposed tax on goods and services coming into a country.

Total costs: All the costs of a firm combined, including rent, payments to workers, interest on borrowed money, etc.

Total revenues: The price of a unit of product or service multiplied by the total number of units sold.

Trade discount: A discount offered to members of a certain industry group.

Trade terms: The conditions under which a sale is made; the period allowed for payment and any discount allowed for early payment.

Transaction costs: Fees or costs incurred when buying and selling goods or services.

Transfer price: The price charged by one segment of an organization for a product or service which it supplies to another segment of the same organization.

Variable costs: Costs that change with the level of production. Such costs are uniform per unit, but fluctuate in total in direct proportion to changes in the related total activity or volume of output.

Wholesalers: Businesses that buy products in large quantities from producers, store them, and resell them in smaller lots to retailers, industrial users, or institutions.

Index

About the Author

Stephen L. Montgomery is president of S. L. Montgomery & Associates, Milwaukee, Wisconsin. His firm provides computer-based management education, management consulting services, and information management services. Mr. Montgomery has experience in a variety of marketing and general management situations ranging from manufacturing companies to retail and service organizations. He is an adjunct faculty member of Cardinal Stritch College and Milwaukee Area Technical College.